Shades of Grey

By

Gary L. Bordelon

authorHOUSE™

1663 LIBERTY DRIVE, SUITE 200
BLOOMINGTON, INDIANA 47403
(800) 839-8640
WWW.AUTHORHOUSE.COM

First published by AuthorHouse 04/13/05

ISBN: 1-4208-2448-1 (sc)

Printed in the United States of America
Bloomington, Indiana

This book is printed on acid-free paper.

Table of Contents

Preface

Through my years in life, I have learned that most police agencies and people are two faced. I'm sure that most police, as I witnessed police corruption in the line of duty. I have also witnessed it not only as a police officer but also as a civilian. I don't wish to hurt any individuals that I have encountered but simply to tell my story.

Chapter One

One-Two-Three Hut!

One-Two-Three Hut!

One-Two-Three Hut!

This is what I heard as I marched to the Louisiana State Police Denn Hall of the police academy. I was in my first week of the academy as an official Louisiana State Policeman. As I marched I immediately heard the comidante say "stop marching trooper" he looked at me and said, "what is your future uniform colors", I said "dark blue pants and light blue shirt" however I also had on light green socks. This pretty well sums up how my state police career went. He told me that I had to run five times around the compound, which came to about five miles. After running a couple laps he told me I could stop.

My entire police career was a whole three and a half years and also a beginning period of high expectations and truthfulness and ended with me in a total state of disillusionment. My beginning police career started, I guess, when I was in college in Monroe, Louisiana. I was a member of the first class that graduated at Northeast College with a degree in Law Enforcement in 1973.

No other school had this degree but Northeast at this time. The intention of this college program for police officers was an attempt to professionalize police officers.

After graduating college, I had a choice of going into the Louisiana State Police in Monroe, Louisiana or to become a lieutenant helicopter pilot in San Antonio, Texas. This was my first bad choice in life. In hindsight, I should have joined the military. However, I did join the Louisiana State Police and going through immediate academy in Baton Rouge, Louisiana. What I mean by immediate is that they had to shorten the academy length to graduate and they needed troopers on the road, as they were short handed. They had not hired any new troopers in a while.

After going through State Police Academy with no problem, I committed an infraction, which I did not report. I was coming home from the academy for the weekend and I had all my uniforms in the back seat to get cleaned. While driving home in my personal car another car passed me at a high rate of speed crossing a double yellow line, nearly causing an accident. After seeing this I grabbed a shirt from the back seat and put it on. I proceeded to chase the car with my flashers on. I finally stopped him ten miles down the road close to a town named Bunkie, Louisiana. The driver pulled over and I got out my car and approached their car and asked them what were they trying to do, kill someone? They immediately smiled at me and showed me their badges, as they were both city policemen from Shreveport, Louisiana. Not knowing what to do I told them that they, of all people, should know how to drive. They politely said that they were sorry but I could not write them a ticket because they were fellow police officers. Later on in my police career, I learned what they meant. What it meant was police officers or their immediate family was not to get a ticket from another police officer. This also meant tickets for speeding only. After police academy, I was sent to Troop F in Monroe, Louisiana. This incident taught me the meaning of the blue code. Whenever you see a fellow officer do something that was not a life or death situation it was "see no evil, say no evil".

1973

Being a rookie state police officer, I had to ride with a veteran police officer the first month. When I got to write my first ticket on the first day, it took me over an hour to write it. The person I was giving the ticket to helped me fill it out. I wrote him a ticket for seventy miles per hour but the veteran I was working with told me to drop the speed to ten miles over the speed limit. He said to give the man a break, the driver was not a nigger but white so I followed orders. We ended up the day by shooting at turtles in a bayou. As in police academy I did not think that was the way things were going to be, but it seemed to work different on the outside. We did not write many tickets while working with this veteran cop because he didn't want to be bothered with possible court. After working with the veteran officer I was put on the road by myself. I got to work days a couple weeks but quickly moved to the evening and midnight shift. I hated these shifts but the challenge seemed to be easier. I had one exciting chase on a stolen car. I chased the car until he ran off the road into a cornfield. He jumped out the car and all I saw was the backside of him. After he fled the car I did another no-no. I shot a warning shot into the air and the suspect fell. I became very nervous because I thought I had jerked the trigger and hit the suspect on accident. While waiting to see what to do, the black suspect got up and started running again. I was glad I didn't hit the suspect and too scared to go chase him. A veteran officer came up behind me and asked if I had shot and I said "yes, I fired a warning shot" which I should not have done and he said don't tell anyone. He then asked me who the driver was and I stated the suspect was black. The veteran officer then told me don't shoot a warning shot just shoot the suspect because he was black. After about fifteen minutes another officer brought the black suspect to me which he had picked up on the road near a cornfield. I told the veteran officer that this young black man was not wearing the same clothes I had witnessed. I could not identify the suspect. The veteran officer said "He's got a little mud on him and he is black, so he will do". He said this would enable me to receive a large lightening bolt decal for the side of my unit to show off how many stolen cars I retrieved. About six months after this incident, I had to go to court for this young man. I didn't feel that he was the suspect that I saw that night because I didn't get a good look at them. I told the judge that was not the suspect I had seen the night before. It seemed to agitate the Assistant District Attorney that I did not help him convict the suspect and he said thy all look alike it would not have hurt to say it was him.

My career in Monroe ended a short time later with a big blunder. I had the usual troubles like running off the road while making a U-turn, and locking my keys in the car while getting out, but this was an easy one. I had trouble staying awake on the midnight shift because it would be deserted some nights, so I thought of away to do something about this. I drove to the nearest interstate by Troop F and started working radar for speeders at about 4 a.m. I fell asleep about 4:15 a.m. and slept until 7:30 a.m. with the sound of my radar waking me up. After waking up I could hear all kinds of units looking for me as well as a helicopter. I immediately drove as fast as I could, without telling anyone that I was all right, to Troop F headquarters. While getting out the car, when it was still running, I had accidentally locked my keys in the car and hit the siren button. The siren got louder and louder. I ran into the troop telling everyone I was all right. After that incident, I ran outside with the maintenance man with vehicle key and he took care of the problem.

I knew I was in trouble but I was only twenty-one years old and didn't know what to do. The captain immediately called me into his office and asked what happened. I simply told him I had fallen asleep and slept through shift change. He told me that I had to do three things to keep from being suspended; he liked my truthfulness so he was going to give me a break. First, I had to get a pocket alarm and set it to go off at 5a.m. second, I had to buy a chain with a spare key to hang around my neck; and thirdly, I had to accept a transfer where there was not a midnight shift to work. I had to either go to Jackson Parish or Tensas Parish in two weeks. I had to work another two weeks all night shifts and the pocket alarm only went off while writing a ticket.

One day as I was working traffic radar at Troop F, I was on a side street in a black section of town to make it easier to write a speeding ticket. I was on a street with a low speed and within a short time I caught a speeder. He was a young black male with a previous speeding violation. Upon stopping him, the driver was well dressed and courteous and immediately handed me his driver's license. He stated that he knew he was going to get a ticket because everyone that was black in this neighborhood would automatically be issued a ticket. I thought to myself that as courteous as he was and if he were a white person would I have given him a ticket. I thought to myself that I would not give him a ticket and I handed his driver's licenses back and he was shocked. This I remember because I saw this driver a week later at the same location he thanked me again and stated the reason he was speeding earlier was because he was a youth minister at the nearby church and he was running late. By my not using discretion gave him a better attitude toward discrimination. He also wanted me to speak to his Sunday school class of teens but I wasn't allowed to. I was not the public relations officer for the troops.

Chapter Two

I chose to transfer to Jonesboro Hodge, Louisiana that is located in Jackson Parish. This was a very good place to work and this is where I really liked state police work. I didn't work in this parish long because I thought the grass was always greener on the other side of the fence.

In talking about the job in Jonesboro, you could not be late when going to work and you could not get off too early. If I had to be at work for 8:00 a.m. and I was running a little late I would simply call the sheriff's department and tell them to contact Troop F and let them know I was on duty already. I always gave the department extra time. I worked just the Jackson Parish so I did not have to go anywhere else. This town was as close to Mayberry in the Andy Griffith Show as you could get. As I was working in Jackson Parish I did learn that the previous two troopers who worked before me in Jackson Parish was asked to leave the parish by the sheriff of the town. After working there about a month, the sheriff asked me into his office and proceeded to tell me he had four of my tickets on

7

his desk that I had issued for traffic violations. He said that I did not make any comments stating that the ticket holder had given me a hard time and if I didn't mind could he fix them. I told him "sheriff my job is to write the ticket and not to prosecute them." I told him that is was his problem because he had to answer to the voters not me. I told him "I don't care what you do with them as long as they don't give me a hard time when issuing a ticket." The sheriff really liked this meeting and he felt he could work with me. The next meeting I had was with the district attorney. I was running around the local high school track and he was running behind me when I glanced at him and he saw me he said, "Wait, I need to talk to you" in a stern voice. I then noticed him trying to catch up. I did not know who he was at the time and I did not have any kind of weapon on me I started running trying to flea him. After about four laps of being chased, neither him nor I could run any longer. I had to stop running and I felt that we were both so tired that we couldn't hurt each other in a fight. He started walking towards me bent over and told me who he was, the district attorney of Jackson Parish. He said that we have a problem with court fund in Jackson Parish and I looked at him and said "What happened, did someone steal it" he started laughing and said that he needed DWI arrests and more tickets. I told him I would do the best I could but I couldn't give a violation where there wasn't one. Myself and one other trooper was the only one in the parish and he averaged one ticket a month so I told him that he should get with the sheriff and they should work something out and to leave me out of this.

The one big thing that happened to me in Jonesboro happened on a very normal Sunday. My wife and I were well liked in the community and all the townsfolk would come by my house and wave and blow the horn.

This is where they would stop sometimes and laugh at my short, dried up watermelon vines. I had about ten of them growing in the front yard. On a particular Sunday I had pulled over a truck filled with watermelons. The truck was definitely in very bad shape and I would have pulled the truck over anyway. After pulling over the truck I told the man that the truck was really overloaded and he should not be using it to drive. I only gave him a warning ticket, which he really appreciated. He then said "trooper let me help relieve the load on this truck" he told me to open my trunk and gave me fifteen watermelons. After getting off work about ten minutes later I drove home and took the watermelons out of the trunk and placed them around the vines in my front yard to make it look like they were growing there. Everyone stopped and looked at the watermelons and could not believe how fast and pretty the watermelons had grown. My friends in the neighborhood would stop and I pretended to cut the watermelon from the vines.

I remember two particular stops in Jonesboro. One dealt with a murder. Two game wardens from Jackson Parish called for help at an old cemetery and I happened to be close by. I started in route to the scene and as I pulled up two officers were on the ground with guns pulled pointed towards the woods. One of the game wardens stated someone was killing from the woods. They did not know his exact whereabouts. I asked if someone was shooting and they said no but they wanted me to get my camera and walk into the woods with them. After walking a little piece I witnessed a man laying on the ground with a tire tool stuck in his forehead with his brains scattered. This made me violently ill and worse matters my wife had meatloaf for supper when I arrive home. I couldn't stand to look at my supper I had to throw it out the back door. One other stop that is vividly in my mind is when I pulled over a drunken driver. After pulling him over instead of getting out of the driver's side he got out on the passenger side and fell down a ten foot embankment into a culvert with water. I could not find him at first but then he started splashing in the water. I asked him what was he doing and he stated he was trying to catch his fish. He had a fifteen-pound fish in his car and it fell out the car along with the driver. He wouldn't come out the water until he got his fish. He got back on the side of the road and said "I know I'm drunk but I couldn't loose my fish" I couldn't arrest him because I had to bring him to the hospital for a broken arm and had his car towed in.

Chapter Three

The worst choice I made in life was when I was talked into accepting a transfer to Region Three as a narcotics investigator for the Louisiana State Police. I couldn't believe how much they wanted me to transfer and how easy it would be to transfer. I though being an investigator in plain clothes would be a step up. Little did I know how wrong I was and how bad a mistake this would be.

The night before we moved from Jonesboro the local community called us and tried to stop us from moving. We received over three hundred phone calls begging us to stay and promised they would support me as in a sheriff campaign within the next four years.

After the current sheriff was retiring in four years I was promised all of their support. I ended up by telling them I had made my decision for my family and I to go back to where we were raised.

I transferred to narcotics in January 1975. My office was in a doublewide trailer. The narcotics section dealt with four field agents to cover Central Louisiana. We had one lieutenant over the region. We had a sergeant that was over four agents in the Alexandria area region. It should be noted that at this time I started narcotics with a friend of mine whom I graduated from high school and college. He also talked me into going into narcotics. I did not know how to dress, what to do, and I surely didn't know what narcotics were like. I had never been around it in all my life.

My first day on the job I was shown what different narcotics looked like and was introduced to my fellow workers. The sergeant was an old veteran from New Orleans, LA who had pretty well lost touch with what was going on. The other two agents in the office were also veterans on the force but I reserve the right to speak of them later.

We were told to go home and come back later that night and we would be given further instructions on what to do. We were instructed to do nothing.

While being at the office the first morning I was given my first official undercover and detective car. I could drive this car home and anywhere else I needed. The car was a very old Pontiac Lemans that was used for prior undercover investigations in the Alexandria area. It was a very unique car in that the police radio that was in the car had been forced into the glove box and the glove box could not be shut. This was a hazard because if anyone sat in the front seat they could see through the crack a police radio that could not be removed from the car. I had to use duct tape to conceal and better close the glove box.

The car was yellow and white and I added black spots to conceal the color and make it look different. The antennae of the car wouldn't stay up so I had to throw it in the trunk. If I wanted to use the radio I would have to jump out the car, get the antennae and screw it down before I could use it. The biggest problem with the car is that the doors were too heavy and they didn't close very well. The muffler was so low to the ground when I hit a bump in the road it would fall off. The muffler came off several times.

I should have known something was wrong when I got into narcotics. I didn't know how easy it was to transfer into narcotics and I didn't know what I was doing. Lastly, receiving the Lemans to go to work in should have warned me of my future plight. After getting our cars, we drove home. I didn't know what to do or when to return to the job. I thought to myself I would go back after dark and I would figure out what came next. My partner was from Alexandria also.

Cain graduated from high school and college with me. You have to believe that Cain and myself were like Starkey and Hutch. Cain had just seen the movie Serpico. He and I naturally thought we were unstoppable. We both left at the same time that night and pulled up to our make shift office which was a doublewide trailer next to Troop E. When we got to the office no one was there and the office was locked. We didn't know how to get in touch with anyone. Cain said he was leaving to go visit with some friends in Pineville. He had some money on him, which was his personal money. I did not see him until the next day. After I left him I drove to the Alexandria Mall for an evening of buying drugs. I had forty dollars on me. I found out that marijuana cost ten dollars for a one-ounce bag. I went into the mall and walked to the center court and sat on a bench. You had to believe that I was the biggest crime fighter around. After sitting on the bench for a short while no one came around the bench. A little while later a couple of guys walked by then walked away then came back to me and asked if I wanted to buy anything. I asked what did he have and he told me a one-ounce bag of marijuana. The guy said he wanted fifteen dollars and I looked at him and said, "I thought it was ten dollars." The guy said o.k. I was just testing you. Throughout the night I kept buying one-ounce bags of marijuana and finally ended up with four ounces from four different people. I had spent forty dollars that evening. I didn't know these people so as I was going to my car I ran them down and asked for their names and phone numbers and they gave that information to me. I told them I wasn't from this area and had no friends so they volunteered the information so I would go back to them.

I got in my car and went home with the marijuana. I thought to myself then that I would grow my hair longer.

The next morning I woke up and found my notebook where I had written down names and numbers of the guys I bought the marijuana from. My partner and I drove to the office to turn in our evidence to the sergeant and collect our money that we used from our personal funds. Come to find out he was only an acting sergeant, the original sergeant could not handle the situation we just proposed to him. I spoke with the sergeant and he told me they would reimburse me the following month when the funds were available but he never did.

The real sergeant told me not to do anything until I had someone else with me. I spent the rest of the month riding around visiting friends. One Friday night I was told that there would be giving a going away party for my sergeant who was leaving for New Orleans. I went to the party at a hotel about two hours after it started. In the mean time I had gotten to know a lot of law enforcement people. When I walked into the party everyone you could name from the area I was working was there.

I was taught and believed up to this point that policemen were to be held at a higher standard. This party was a reality check for me. A girl informant that was very nice looking was completely naked dancing with the regional director of the FBI. Most everyone was drunk and policemen were in different areas of the ballroom drinking and with other women. I immediately wanted to leave which I did. However, in the parking lot was a state police detective about to fight with the assistant chief of the Alexandria Police Department. I had observed him earlier at a burglar scene taking a lot of rare coins that was blamed on the suspect that had broken into the place. The detective of the state police put his hands in his back pockets and dared the assistant chief to hit him. The state policeman was known to be hot tempered. Both men were drunk and nose to nose yelling at each other. After putting his hands in his back pockets, he begged the assistant chief to hit him. This went on for about three minutes finally the assistant chief hit the state policeman in the face. This was his mistake because the state policeman looked at the assistant chief laughing and said, "Is this all you got, I was tired of begging you to hit me." He then took his hands from his pockets and threw the assistant chief on the ground and was standing over him hitting him in the face. Finally after a few minutes other policemen stopped them. They all went back inside drinking the rest of the night. I left and went home. I didn't know what else to do.

Chapter Four

In order to best tell the complete story of how I feel and how I was abused mentally and emotionally by the state of Louisiana where I worked undercover, the first city I will talk about is Leesville, Louisiana.

As I started working undercover narcotics I did not have long hair so I did not fit the bill in the drug culture as a longhaired hippy. I had to work with the detective division of the state police Region 3 and the CID at Fort Polk. I had to dress as an Army guy from Fort Polk who had a weekend pass. I called a cab and told him to drive me to the crossings. This was a place about a block in size that dealt with prostitution and drugs that Fort Polk soldiers visited. It had a pool hall with women standing around waiting for guys. In normal black individuals they were dressed as pimps. I was to drive to the area in a cab and look as if I were a soldier. I was wired so detectives could listen in on the conversations that I would be having. I was not to make any prostitution cases but soliciting cases so the women would offer me sexual favors and once they named their price the case was made. They would not be arrested until the end of the week during a round up. I did this for about three nights and made about forty soliciting cases until the night before we were to make the round up. I made anywhere from forty to fifty cases of different women until that Thursday night. Thursday I started my same routine and one girl came up to me stating she recognized me from previous nights. She said she wasn't going to talk to me because she thought I was weird. She said you are playing games because you never want to follow through with anything. I thought to myself I would try something different. I told her I could get a cheaper price that one prostitute named "Toni" said I can get a fucky sucky for $15 and you want $15 for a fucky only. The prostitute went by a different name each time and said "that bitch should not be undercutting other's prices". She then told me she would give me a fucky sucky for $10 to undercut Toni. When Toni heard this she said she would do both for $7. The next thing I know they had jumped on the each other and were fighting on the sidewalk and rolled onto the street then five or six more prostitutes were fighting. It all looked like a brawl. The guy that was the pimp walked out to stop the fight and he lost his big pink pretty hat in the street then he was mad. I looked for my partner that went with me and said we better get running. We ran as long and as hard as we could and while doing so looked at about forty whores chasing us begging us to stop. After getting out of sight. We were picked up by detectives and brought back to the meeting place to discuss the next day's preparation for a round up. With the amount of cases I made, and other officers working, charges on over one hundred people. Now this place, deep in my mind, was one of the best places for a young soldier to go. All the girls apparently had the same attorney's name to call in case of trouble.

As Friday night started we were ready to do the round up and everyone had a plan of what they were suppose to do. I was picked as the only one to go back undercover with a wire attached to make a real prostitution case. That would mean going back to their room after they disrobed and I started to disrobe they were suppose to tell me the price. I was then supposed to give them the money and then show them my badge. Before I left the staging place we synchronized our watches. I was going to have five minutes head start so I could leave the area to make the prostitute case. Somehow the raid started too soon as we were going into her trailer. When the prostitute saw all the police cars in the area I pretended I did not know what was going on because I was afraid of what would happen once in the trailer. Before we could close the door of the trailer she said "get out of here white boy we are all going to jail together if they see you in here." I said "Toni, what do you want me to do." I then told her I was leaving and she said "hurry get the fuck out of here". I opened the trailer door and four more black prostitutes ran into the trailer with us. Someone yelled to me "who are you, the police" and I said "no I'm trying to get out the trailer" and Toni said, "no he ain't no police, he is a fool from Fort Polk". All the prostitutes ran into the closet. I said to Toni "I can't leave now with all the cops and besides we still have time to do something" since I already paid her. I asked Toni if I could have a refund since we wouldn't be able to do anything. I said to the prostitutes "Y'all have to help me" as I tried to get in the closet with them. Try to imagine five people in a small clothes closet. Everyone was being quite. I said, "I can't breathe in here. Y'all have to hide me better because I don't want to get in trouble at the base." Toni said "be quite for a while until the police leave." After a short time I farted. The prostitutes said "that's it, now we will go to jail stinking".

One of the prostitutes said the smell would pass eventually but the smell wasn't going away. It was crowded and stuffy in the closet but I wasn't going to tell them I was a police officer so I told them to be quite so no one would hear us. One told me if you would get out the closet we would have enough room. I then opened the closet door a little bit and heard a knock on the trailer door asking if anyone was in the trailer. I replied by saying "No one is here whoever you are" but I knew all along it was the police. One of the prostitutes in the closet pulled me back into the closet and closed the door. She says "Are you crazy fool, don't answer them". The trailer door then opened and another guy who identified himself as a police officer came into the trailer. The officer said, "is anyone here" and I looked at the prostitutes and saw we were sweating pretty bad and I yelled back "no one is in here officer". After hearing that Toni told me "shut up stupid, now they will know we are here." The police then pulled his pistol and demanded everyone out the closet or I will start shooting. "Don't shoot officer I have to pull up my pants and then I will be out." As we all came out the closet one of the prostitutes said, "you sure are stupid saying nobody was here." We were all handcuffed and brought to the maintenance center for booking.

All the people that worked with me in my section began to laugh and then unhand cuffed me. I said, "why didn't one of y'all want to do this and why did you show up so early". After arriving at the booking center Toni said, "I know what you really want" she then pulled her pants down and mooned me. They all used one prominent lawyer from Rapides Parish who handled their deals. He is still an attorney in this town and according to reports only a few were ever prosecuted. All I know is I never went to court to testify about anything.

19

A second time I went undercover in Leesville I had to work just downtown with another agent sort of freelancing. We tried to buy drugs from mostly Army personnel as per our instructions. We worked about two nights and it lasted until the second night. On this night we were in a bar with a bunch of Army guys who were clean cut. I had long hair then and really didn't fit in. They kept asking me for drugs instead of them having any. It ended on the second night when a Fort Polk soldier and three of his buddies walked out on the sidewalk in front of the bar. They were supposed to sell me something. Then when I pulled out my money the first one hit me knocking me to the sidewalk. The other three started jolly stomping me. I pulled my gun that I kept in my boot and when they seen this they backed off. Instead of arresting them and blowing my cover I told them to "get the hell away from me."

The third time I was undercover in Leesville, this happened towards the end of my narcotics career. I had to work undercover with a blond motorcycle gang girl. She told the other people that I was her old boyfriend from way back, so I rode with the gang. She said that the hardest thing would be to be accepted by the rest of the motorcycle gang, however, it wasn't hard for me. In fact the first night of the gang meeting me I was accepted by them.

I had to use an old Harley motorcycle for undercover or an old Falcon car. The Falcon was in terrible condition but the Harley was in worse shape, as it didn't have any brakes. I didn't find this out until I drove to the camp where they had a bonfire. The blond motorcycle girl wants an informant and immediately jumped on back of my motorcycle and said "we are going to have fun tonight, there is a bonfire at the end of this road." She told me the whole motorcycle gang would be there. I told her that it be best if you go to the bonfire ahead of me in her car and let the group know I would be coming behind you to visit. I waited about thirty minutes then I started my motorcycle driving pretty fast headed for the bonfire. It was sort of at a dead end road on top a small hill. I could see the fire approximately thirty yards away and as I traveled pretty fast down the hill I tried to stop and I didn't have any brakes and I started hollering for everyone to get out the way I'm crazy. I flew right through the bonfire and became airborne toward the creek bed and landed in pine thickets. It was dark so I started feeling around on my body to see just what if anything was broken. After knowing I was alright just a little scratched up I hollered "Yee Ha, let's do it again." I could hear the gang saying who is that crazy son-of-a-bitch, I could hear the blond motorcycle girl say, "Oh, that's my old boyfriend." She said "if he's alright when he gets up the hill, I'm going to put a hump in his back". So when I heard this I crawled up the hill and pretended that my leg was hurt but that it would be all right later. The gang offered me a beer and offered me a rope so I could pull my bike back up the hill. One of the gang helped me fix my wheel and partial brakes as he sold me some acid. I made narcotic distribution cases from about six of the gang members the next day. They had an assortment of drugs that I could buy like pills, marijuana, cocaine, etc. After buying from six different people I had to keep the drugs separate so I could tag them later as to what I bought from what individual.

As I said the gang members partially fixed my brakes as long as I slowed down before my stop. As I was riding down the highway with the blond girl on the back she was a good informant but very tomboyish and aggressive. I kept having to tell her to quit grabbing my crotch because it took all I had to keep the bike up. No more than ten miles out of town a policeman came up behind us and pulled us all over. Well after not having time to down shift I tried to put on the brakes and they didn't catch. What it looked like to the officer was that everyone stopped but me. He thought I was trying to get away because I pulled on the shoulder but couldn't stop. After turning off the bike and coasting about two hundred yards onto the shoulder and using my boots to help me stop the officer had forgotten about the rest of the gang and came after me. The officer immediately pulled me off the motorcycle, slammed me against his car, pulled my wallet out and retrieved my licenses he then took the blonde's licenses. The officer discovered a warrant out for her arrest so he handcuffed her and she thought the officer wouldn't do anything to her because she was an informant and she knew we promised to get her out. She went along with the situation peacefully, however when they got to me they started patting me down and they found all the drugs I had on me plus a switchblade in one boot and an undercover gun in the other boot along with a lot of money. To top it all off the motorcycle at one time or another had been stolen. I could not tell the officer who I really was so they immediately threw me to the ground and charged me with numerous violations. I had one number to call to be bonded out which was another agent but as usual he was at a family function. I had to sit in jail overnight and plead for another phone call before I got bonded out. When the police took all the evidence, knife, and gun it was destroyed. I got the gun and knife back. After this I started using a car but the blond was so rough talking she had tattoos all over her and everyone she knew didn't have much money or much to say to her. After meeting most of her friends I kept asking her to buy something big after a two week period I made about fifteen cases of distribution of various drugs from various people. I was just about ready to pull out because of other places calling for me, and then she took me to someone who was supposed to have a pretty good variety of drugs to sell. I met up with her and naturally she had to ride like she always did with no shirt on. We went to a house out of town and something told me I didn't like this place but I made her stay in the car. The blond suggested I go on in someone was waiting in there for me. I had about $2,000. on me to buy the drugs and I walked through the front room to the kitchen where the person was and it was dimly lit. I could see that the person had one arm under the table that let know he probably had a gun under the table. I walked up to him and asked if he had some stuff to sell. He then said "Put your money on the table if I don't have the drugs now I'll get you some." I then said "It don't work that way. I'm not leaving my money. You contact the blond when you do have some." I then heard what sounded like a trigger being cocked on a gun, but what he didn't know; I already had my right hand behind my back with my gun. The situation being like it was I knew he was going to rob me. I immediately pulled my gun around and fired at him, hitting him in the neck area. With the force of shot, he fell to the floor. I then walked around the table to see if I had killed him but he appeared to be unconscious and very little blood. This was very unnerving so I jumped in my car and went to meet the agent I was working for. After telling him what had occurred he advised me not to tell anyone unless we found out for sure he was dead. Someone checked on the man later and he was all right. The agent then told me the next day we would terminate the investigation. With the three different undercover duties I made in Leesville none of the cases were prosecuted, except one black boy that I had bought $5. Marijuana from. With this you can pretty much see how the legal system was in Vernon Parish. I was giving a lot of money to use and it was an easy system used as to where I spent it. I can say that it seems to be funny that on the last night when the boy was shot the blond I was working with asked me in a puzzling sense what was it doing me to be back at the car. Makes you wonder what was really suppose to happen.

Beauregard Parish

Like I stated earlier, the different times that I worked in different places was not in chronological order it was just continuous. In two and a half years I only remember the first undercover place and the last. The sheriff of Beauregard Parish, which included Deridder, was constantly calling for me to come work undercover. He wanted me to bring another agent with me and that he had a good informant to work with. This informant is supposed to know everyone around. Well, we had three basic problems, one the informant was very easy going and easy to get along with but with all the people he knew they were wondering how he was able to get out of jail with all the charges he had on him. He also had a girlfriend that was underage; second - the general terrain was very country and it wasn't much of a city to go to as the parish was dry; thirdly - the people were very hard to get along with because of them being so clamish. However, even with all this the sheriff after meeting us and seeing how I looked appearance wise he said I have to have you. He knew I could get drugs from anybody.

I looked like a drug head. He gave us a lot of money to work with but gave us very poor living conditions. He put us in an old camp that belonged to a friend of his that was located by a big lake in this parish. The place was in the wilderness and we had to drive a long way back into town. There were no stores within ten miles and we saw very little people around. You could walk around the woods naked for days without being seen. We fought over were we would sleep at this camp that was also the home to roaches and snakes. There was very little food so we were constantly driving back into the town for food. We had no refrigerator and no litreen. We would leave every morning from the camp going to try and talk with the informant's friends. We tried just about anything to get in with people. We made a few marijuana cases where you would smoke pot and one of the agents would hold the roach, which is the butt to get the distribution charge. The agents only simulated smoking. This is always how we testified which was total horseshit. We made about six cases in two weeks. We met with the sheriff again he knows that we can do better and he asked if sometimes I could go out on my own, so I did that and made eight cases in three nights. It was obvious the informant was jacking us around. After another talk with the informant we all struck out again. We made just a few more cases but I was beginning to think the undercover investigation would take somebody to have a job where people could see you and become to know them. Two things ended the investigation. The first time we went to a teenage skating rink, which the informant was begging to do, was to see his girlfriend who was just a teenager herself. Immediately after going into the building the owner of the place looked at us and thought we were there to rob the place. The girlfriend's dad was there. It turned into a big brawl and we were chased out the skating rink. Shortly after leaving the skating rink down the road a deputy pulled us over. The deputy saw that we were drinking and we were caught with drugs which was evidence of the two cases that were made earlier in the night. We didn't know whether to tell the deputy the truth who we really were. The informant, after being handcuffed, looked at us as our guns were being found and seeing us getting handcuffed started hollering. He looked at my partner and me and asked us in a loud panicky voice that he thought we were real cops. I then told the deputy to dig further in my boot and he would find my identification and badge. He said after finding it "I'm sorry" and he removed the handcuffs and looked at the informant and said "This is why you aren't in jail yet because you were and informant." We had to contact the sheriff and tell him what had taken place and the sheriff was to contact the deputy to keep quite. The last time happened in one day. We were back at the roach infested camp and we had just gotten up and the next thing we knew a whole team of deputies raided us at the camp. They were there to investigate camp burglars and they were told we were not from this area and that we were probably the ones that were doing the burglaries. The informant started running which didn't make it look good so we started walking back into the camp. They found pistols, knives, and drugs and were also charging us with a possible homicide. The deputies called in our undercover names and my rap sheet seemed to be very bad. What saved us was the deputy that early on had arrested us while leaving the skating rink a couple days before. He contacted the sheriff and the sheriff in turn contacted the supervisor and told him to let us go and for the deputy to get his ass back to the office. I said you need to remember that undercover investigations was needed either before elections or after elections and I don't think the sheriff trusted his deputies too much. I contacted the sheriff and told him that he had a better set up closer to town. I would be able to do a better job. I went back to the camp to tell the others and my partner, who wasn't a very good undercover and dying to go home, that it was over and we needed to get our stuff and leave. While I was gone my partner wanted to cook dinner instead of going into town. He found can goods of pork-n-beans and made some red beans and rice. This doesn't seem to be important but all I ate was a small bowl of pork-n-beans and walked out the back door. I looked around and everything was spinning and I started throwing up. He asked me what was wrong and I asked him was something wrong with the food and he said, "no it didn't smell bad, but the cans seemed to be rounded on both ends. I said, "You poisoned me mother fucker" I got in the car, he drove and we left the informant. We drove of speeds well in access of 100 mph so I could get to a hospital in our office town to have my stomach pumped. I was nearly unconscious. When I left the hospital I went home to rest and hid my car so they would not send me on another undercover assignment. I was the number one agent on everyone's list.

Red River Parish

My very first undercover investigation when they put me by myself was in Red River Parish. The owner of the place knew who I was because he was friends with the detective that I had to report in to. I was set up to work at a big truck stop to work of big trucks. The first week I had trouble making any cases because I would live in an air-conditioned motel room that they didn't know about. Finally, the patrolman told me I had to live in an abandoned trailer that had no air conditioner or running water. I lived there for about three weeks. After a while I started getting in with everyone and made a few cases mainly from the truck stop. One of the ladies at the truck stop was selling speed to the truckers and you have to know in this area most of the people were what you called "high yeller" people. I was getting along very well and everything was pointing to one black couple. The black guy went by the name Cowboy. Cowboy was selling most of the marijuana. I had made friends with some of the black people in the area. We drove to Cowboy's house not realizing he was selling the marijuana. The first night he would only sell us a small amount because he wanted to see us smoke the pot. I had to simulate smoking and I got so messed up that I drove down a two-lane highway on the right shoulder thinking it was a gravel road. Cowboy seemed to like me and invited me back anytime I wanted to. I waited a week before going back. In this time period I got fired three times from the truck stop. One time I went to see my good friend Henry at the other station. The second time I would not pump the amount of diesel in a customer's truck. The third time was when a Dominic's Auction truck full of cows pulled in to fuel and I refused to fuel him. The driver pulled out a pipe from the truck and walked to the back of the truck and stared hitting his tires. He wanted me to fix five flats. I then walked around the trailer and started hitting tires too. I then told him I would not fix this flat, or this flat as I was pointing to the flat tires. After doing this he went to the manager of the truck stop who was the son-in-law of the owner. After repeating what I told him I was fired once again. The manager said, "We don't need drug heads working here and I am tired of firing you." The owner of the truck stop hired me back and I reported in for work the next day. The manager, after seeing me back at work, said, "I'm going to get rid of you one way or the other". I went back out to Cowboy's and bought some marijuana from him and that was the first time I ever saw someone ring up the marijuana purchase in a cash register. I went back another time and Cowboy wasn't there so his wife sold me some and rang it in the cash register. After this I started making a lot more cases, as people would come by and sell to me and I was running fencing operation at the station buying stolen items. Then one day I went to a bar close to where I worked and this dark complexioned guy came up to me and sold me a pistol. He had about eight of his buddies around. He said, "you are the only new comer around here and we have been having a lot of burglaries." Something wasn't right. After getting back to the station, in which I was running late from my lunch break, two deputies pulled up from Red River Parish. They started questioning me about all the things around the station. They then arrested me for twenty-one counts of burglary and found the gun in my boot. They brought me to jail where I stayed for four days because the guy I was to report to was on vacation. They gave me several lie detector tests in which I failed them all. I had gotten into many fights in the jail but finally they allowed me a phone call after four days. I called my contact to come bail me out. He showed up to have me released. After getting out and I'm back at the station I was riding around one night and I pulled into a rest area. There was a van parked with three guys and one girl who weren't from the area. After talking to them a little while they showed me drawing about how to make bombs. They asked if I would spend the night with them. They had no money and I was leery of them. I took them to a local store and they must have shoplifted $50 -$100 worth of groceries. When I stayed and watched this they began to trust me and showed me their plans to bomb different places and all the different drugs they had. They had numerous sheets of acid, marijuana, and heroin. They asked me if I would like to join them as they were using these drugs and I told them no. I was already messed up and I just needed some sleep. They wanted to know if I would buy some drugs from them and I told them I was broke but that I had a friend in Alexandria, LA who would buy from them. I called the police friend in Alexandria and set them up to meet so they would get busted in Alexandria and not in Red River Parish. I gave them the phone number to call my friend and $20 for gas to get there. They went to Alexandria and they were busted and it turned out to be one of the biggest terrorist busts in Alexandria at that time. I knew it would not bother me working undercover but what it caused was they sending me one of the first black state undercover officers so I could train him. I took the new recruit around a few places and he was scared to death. I then took him to Cowboy's place. Again we purchased marijuana and again it was ringed up in the cash register. A little while later the new recruit was so messed up he lay in the front seat and passed out. I knew the undercover investigation was over so I went to a bar that most everyone hung out in that area and I was surrounded by a motorcycle gang. They said they thought I was a cop and they were out to kill me but I was leaning against my car on the passenger side. Somehow immediately hearing this my recruit pulled out his pistol and pointed at them and said "First one touches my white friend will be shot." They backed up and that was the end of that episode. The next day to end the investigation, I went back to the truck stop to work and again I was two hours late. The manager came straight up to me and told me once again I was fired. I told him to fuck himself and I left town. We had to go back to Red Ricer Parish one more time to testify and I never saw any person get 17 years for 2 counts of distribution of marijuana like Cowboy did. The black officer came with me and he was scared to death. The funniest thing happened as we were leaving we had a blow out which sounded like a gunshot. My black friend hid under the dash and I laughed as he thought we were being shot at. He never got out the car he was too scared. I had to change the flat.

New Roads

I had just returned from an undercover investigation and I knew I needed to rest. I was really tired but they promised my services to work in New Roads, LA. The people I met with from the sheriff's department said that we needed to really do something that things were really bad. The informant I was to work with had worked in a service station in town and the owner of the station was to hire me when I came looking for a job. I was forced out the car bare footed and old ragged clothes and I was told to walk to the station. I did have a lot of money on me to buy drugs, which came from the sheriff's department. I walked to the station a couple blocks away, trying to avoid the hot concrete from burning my feet. When I got to the station, the owner took me to the back and told me I needed shoes to work there and then preceded to question me about being sure I was the correct man. I said, "Look it's me and give me this old pair of rubber boots". The station owner agreed to hiring me but told me I would have to work like everyone else. After meeting a few people the informant knew I knew right then that I didn't feel like going through another case again. I just wanted to go home and rest.

The first night my sleeping quarters consisted of an old automobile hood. I couldn't sleep in the informant's home because of the flea and rodent condition of the house.

After reporting to the station at 7:00 a.m. I said, "This investigation has ended". I had not had a shower in about three days so I knew whom I had to bust. That evening the informant did not return to work because he was cooking a batch of crystal methanphetamine. I got to my sleeping quarters early because the station owner had fired me. I wasn't paying attention and I had started a gas fire at the station. The owner said, "I don't believe you are who you say you are. You are nothing more than a dope head like everyone else." I asked him not to fire me but if he insisted may I please use his truck to go to my friends. He said "Get the hell out of here now before I call the police". I left immediately. When I arrived at the informant's house he had a string of people waiting in line to buy the crystal he had been cooking all day. I knew then I needed to make a case on my informant. I told him I had gotten fired. The informant then asked me if I was really a policeman. I told him that I don't know who I am any more but I knew I was crazy and sleepy. Before I left I asked the informant if I could buy some crystal from him. He told me yes and he asked me if I wanted him to rig it up for me by putting the crystal in a needle. I told him no that I had something in the car. He asked me when was I coming back because he wanted to hurry and sell all the crystal he had that night. After getting something to eat, I drove back to the informant's house and as I pulled into the driveway other search warrants was there from another local police department. I thought to myself here we go again as the informant and myself were handcuffed. Before we left the house a sheriff pulled in and got he pulled me aside with the other policemen and told them I was a real state trooper and not a snitch. They said "Hell with that, they have been cooking crystal all day and he was helping them." I then pulled from my hair the two eight balls of crystal I had purchased from my good informant. I said I was at the station working up until thirty minutes ago when I got fired. The sheriff said that's all now I guess everyone in this town will know who he is. The sheriff knew that the other policemen would tell who I was. I gave the sheriff his money back all but $600.00 that I used to buy the crystal. I told the sheriff if he had something else for me to do I would come back. I really wasn't serious about that statement. I was so glad to be getting home. When I got home my sergeant in Region III said you really know how to end an investigation when you want to. The sergeant showed me his itinerary for the next ten places. He wanted me to work undercover for them and they wanted me to go as far as other states. I told him I was going home for a few days to rest.

Looking back at this investigation, the police that accused me of cooking crystal searched me and couldn't find any drugs on me. He failed to find the eight crystal balls I had stuck in my hair. He kept saying, "I don't know how he pulled it off, I know I have searched him."

Catahoula Parish

The sheriff of Catahoula Parish, I found him to be a very nice man but he was in trouble at election time. He really needed some narcotic cases. I wanted to do the best job I could for him. This was a small town, Jonesville, which was the biggest city in the parish and they were quite clamish. I brought an informant with me from Alexandria because I couldn't find anyone else to go. They said I frightened them. The first night I brought an informant with me so I would have someone to talk to. The second night I brought four more informants with me. We were going to a dance and the informants could move across the dance floor. I thought one of us would get lucky and catch someone selling drugs. Well the building that the dance party was at was adjacent to a restaurant. One of my informants was very pretty. In fact if he were a woman he would have been beautiful. The pretty informant suggested we move to a big table with a big tablecloth that would touch the floor. We all sat down to order our food and Pretty Boy looked at me and said "I bet you I can get a head job from the waitress". She was a heavyset woman that was waiting on us. Pretty Boy said, "Watch, I will continue to look at her and smile. She will look back at me eventually" and she did. He was the last to order his food. However, he was the first to get his dinner and we were still waiting. She told us our dinner would be along shortly. Pretty Boy asked the waitress if he could have his dessert. The waitress came up to where he was sitting and he told her he had strong feeling for her. Pretty boy said to her "if you care about me like I care about you, you would give me a blow job." Pretty Boy pulled out his dick in the restaurant and she looked at him and said "o.k. let me crawl under the table so no one will see me." The rest of us watched and seen the satisfaction on his face. Pretty Boy said to her "here it comes don't get anything on me because we have to go to the dance." She then whispered to us that we could all have the same thing. We all pulled out our dicks and pointed them under the dinner table. I was going to be second in line but I knew Pretty Boy had the claps. She looked at mine and said, "you haven't been circumcised" I told her I didn't want to participate anyway so take the next fellow. She gave all the rest of the informant's blowjobs. You could see the excitement on their faces even as the owner of the restaurant walked up to our table. He said, "y'all seem to be happy, y'all must have had a good meal." I said to him "you couldn't ask for better service." Everyone started laughing except for the last informant who was in the middle of getting his blowjob. She said his dick was too short and skinny. I guess it was too hard for her to grab and her jowls were worn out. She then asked me where her boss was. I told her he went outside. She said, "I have to hurry and get away from this table. Let me go get y'alls food. She came right back out with the food and we could tell she had not washed her face or hands because she had all the evidence of what she had been doing all over her. The plates were sticking to her hands. She put the food on the table and we all got up and left. We told her we had lost our appetite. I asked the waitress if she had done this often and she said she would do it often if she liked someone. I left her a good tip and she told me she would be getting off work after the dance if we wanted to try it again. I told her "no that's alright we have had enough." We went on to the dance. On the way to the dance Pretty Boy told us he had the claps and that he caught it from a gay guy in Alexandria. Everyone started hollering for penicillin pills that Pretty Boy had on him to treat his claps. He gave everyone some but me because I told them I had ethics because I was a police officer. We went on over to the dance and scattered about trying to meet people. The only person who could do me any good with meeting people was Pretty Boy. He had met the lead singer of the band's girlfriend. I said, "oh no here we go, this might be trouble." After the band took a recess the singer's girlfriend went to him and asked him if he would sell us some drugs. The singer left the building and Pretty Boy and myself followed him. Everyone that was in the band had a room rented in the nearby area. We went to the singer's room and bought a bag of marijuana. We then went to the drummer's room and bought a bag of marijuana. We also hit the lead guitar's room and bought a bag from him. Every bag cost me $12 each because every parish North of Rapides, no matter what the cost of the drugs, always put a $2 surcharge on every bag bought. The band members had to hurry back to the stage. They left all their rooms and we all headed back to the dance. When we passed the lead singer's room his girlfriend came out the room in just her panties. She said for us to come on in her room. I asked her what she had in mind, as she was a nice looking girl. I said, "Well I'm really looking for another bag of marijuana. I'm not interested in doing anything with you." She sold me another bag of marijuana and then gave me her calling card and said she could get me a lot more. I told her I was gay. After purchasing the marijuana I went to the dance but before I left I told Pretty Boy to make it quick because I didn't want him to get caught. Well this slightly changed the investigation because he did get caught. I tried to rush all my informants from the dance and we made it as far as my car. The band and locals in the town surrounded us and said politely they would whip our ass.

I looked around the car and I didn't see Pretty Boy he had started walking down the road and they had not noticed him walking away. The oldest informant that was with me was in his 50's. He didn't like taking commotion form anyone. He said "I will whip any of you punk's ass if you touch me". He was the first one hit while standing behind the car. After getting hit we all laughed at the way he fell. He bounced backwards all the way down the car until he got to the front of the car. Falling backward he might not have landed on the ground but he grabbed the hood arm and it gave way. Upon his fall he stuck himself in the eye and carried a black eye for weeks. The rest of the gang proceeded to jump on us but the police arrived. All my informants and myself got arrested except for Pretty Boy who had walked away. The police took us to the station and I told them who I was and what we were doing. They gave me back my marijuana that I had purchased and let us all go after talking to the sheriff. We go out and started home and at least half the crowd was still at the dance. When we passed them we hollered at them and told them better luck next time. Y'all will get arrested because we told the police everything. They all scattered after that.

After driving about ten miles down Hwy. 28 back toward Pineville, we picked up sorry ass Pretty Boy.

The sheriff of Catahoula Parish still needed help, as we did not stop the drug flow into his parish. I had to go one more time and I brought another agent with me with less experience. After talking to the sheriff and the people in the area I learned that the biggest dealer went by the nickname Rooster. I asked the sheriff to drive me to where Rooster lived and then we turned around and got in my car. I told him to work surveillance and I would go in and buy something from Rooster. I drove up to Rooster's old wooden framed house and his mother answered the door. I told her I needed to speak to Rooster and she told me he was in the LaSalle Parish jail in Jena, LA. I told her I had driven a long way and he would have the stuff here for me. She didn't act surprised. She said "Oh the marijuana, its in the back. Come along I will take you back there." Her husband was lying on the bed with a shotgun. He said he had been sick but that no policeman would inter this house for he could smell them a mile away. I then said, "If there is any police involved I don't want to buy any of this because I don't want to be in trouble." He then asked his wife to bring him the box that contained the marijuana bags. She said, "We know Rooster likes you. We will look through the bags and find you the best one." They searched through about fifty to sixty bags and said to me "These are the prettiest three". I paid him $30 because he was dropping the excise tax of $2 per bag. He said as soon as Rooster gets out we will start rolling properly. I couldn't leave there without eating a piece of homemade pie and a big glass of ice tea. I told them I would see them later. I drove back to the sheriff's department and the sheriff asked me "what will we do now". I said, "I'm a police and I saw the stuff. Let me get a search warrant from my brief case and I'll type it up for you." I left to go home. The sheriff got his crew and they ran a search warrant on Rooster's house. The sheriff called me the next day and gave me an acclamation. He said he had been trying to crack that drug case for years.

Colfax

I worked Colfax on three separate occasions. The sheriff and I got along pretty good. He said he didn't have any deputies to work narcotics. I had met him on previous occasions in Rapides Parish. This will be discussed later in the book.

The first time I went to work with him we met up with some people who had been living out of town but had moved back to Grant Parish. At this time I purchased a small quantity of marijuana from them but they showed me a suitcase full in bricks. I told them I had not brought enough money with me but I would meet them the following day at 6:00 p.m. at a certain place. I drove back to meet them but no other policeman would come with me because they were scared. I walked into the residence and said "Exactly how much money will I need to buy the bricks of marijuana from you." They started laughing and said, "That's right we forgot to tell you." All I remember is they said something in the $20 thousands. I left the house and wrote down the address as I was leaving so I could get a search warrant. Again I had to type a search warrant because there wasn't anyone available that knew how to do it. Meanwhile, the sheriff was rounding up a posse. I handed the search warrant to the sheriff and said, "Y'all go get them." The sheriff looked at me and said, "Why aren't you going." I said, "I don't want them to see my face. It might ruin anything I had to do in the future." This bust turned out to be the biggest bust the sheriff's department had made.

The second time I went to work was during the Pecan Festival. The sheriff wanted me to walk around the crowd. I had brought another agent with me to see if we could find anyone who might be selling or using narcotics. We got a first class meal before we started from the jail. Before leaving the jail, someone in jail handed me a joint of marijuana. I didn't have the heart to tell the sheriff so I flushed it down the toilet before leaving the courthouse. We walked the streets until midnight and wasn't able to find anything. Then around 12:30 a.m. a car sideswiped another car by the door and continued driving. The young officers I was training wanted me put the red light on top of our car and go chase the vehicle. I told him that being in a Camero looking like we do you think those people would have pulled over for us. A Grant Parish marked car had caught up with the vehicle and it was in the ditch. The deputy yelled at us why were we at the scene, so I told him we were witnesses and I pulled out my badge. The deputy asked why were we working this case. He said its already been handled it was just ole Bobby and it would not have been an accident to start with but the other driver opened her door causing him to hit her and he panicked. My partner started saying, "That's not how the story goes." I then put my hand over his mouth. I whispered to him that I would talk to the sheriff about it later.

The third time I worked Colfax, I went with three informants and myself. This was more like a search mission so we could find something because we didn't have anything set up. We walked up to a black bar. We were the only white people there. Instead of acting loudly and trying to be seen, I told them to be quite and just mingle. One of the informants, as soon as we got into the parking lot, asked a black guy who seemed to have known of us from Alexandria, did he want to buy some window pane acid. This acid was made of a plastic jug cut into small squares and wrapped with scotch tape. I immediately grabbed the acid from my informant and told him black people don't like acid and don't try to sell any more to them. The black guy kept on antagonizing me and saying y'all were trying to sell me some dope that wasn't real. I told him let's just forget it we will go on about our business and that my informant didn't know what he was doing. The main black defendant who started the whole thing kept on until we found ourselves like punching bags. They knocked all the informants teeth out hitting him from one person to the next. I thought I was going to get away but a big heavy set black got out a pulp wood truck and came over and hit me right in the face closing my right eye. We then broke loose and crawled on our hands and knees back to where our car was. While running I could see small balls of flame passing me. It must have been bullets. The two informant hit the ground fast and yelled to me "Where is your gun don't you have one.

I pulled my gun and started shooting warning shots back into the crowd of blacks. They started scattering. I recognized the guy who shot at me he was a black guy with a turban on his head. I didn't have anyone to call but Pop Hattaway and he told me to wait at the courthouse. Pop Hattaway was sending me reinforcements right away. We then went out in a long line of police cars and raided the nightclub. At first I showed him the guy that shot at me who was the club owner. Then sitting at the table was the main guy who instigated the fight acting as nice as he could be. I grabbed him by his shirt and threw him over a table. He and I started fist fighting and it seemed like I might have been loosing so I reached in my back pocket for a pair of brass knuckles. I then swung at him from behind and hit him in back of his head and he then fell to the floor. I hid the knuckles real fast. The deputies placed him under arrest and took him to the Grant Parish jail. After righting my reports, he hollered at me "I know I can beat you up. You cheated." I said to him "You see where you are so you tell me who won." He then said to me "I'll see you in Alexandria again." When I got to my office the next morning my sergeant asked me about this episode so I told him. By this time my police attitude had changed a lot. I asked my sergeant what he wanted to know about it and he said just tell me the story and I'll go tell the major. He came back a short time later and told me the person he talked to said you just as well leave it alone and that I wasn't shot or killed so don't write up needless paperwork.

Winnfield

I never was officially signed to work in Winnfield. They had assigned another agent to work the area. The undercover agent worked a whole month and only made one case and a got a busted lip. The agent's lip was busted by having doggy style sex with a girl from the Winnfield Hospital. He spent most of his time at the hospital to see the girl every night. The supervisor asked me to go with him one Friday evening and we got there before dark. I also brought another undercover agent with me. I could see the undercover that was already there was very nervous for lack of production. I told him to drive me to where the black bars were in town, which seemed to be one street and they were all located down this one street. I told everyone to get out the car so we could go party. The useless informant was scared and acted like he didn't want to get out. I again asked him to get out so we could meet some people. After getting in the bar, I was swinging the pool stick like a baseball bat and playing loud music. A short time latter three black men came up to one and me had an arm sling on. I could see a small caliber pistol hidden in his arm sling. He seemed to always want to put his good hand down in the sling. I immediately told him to loosen up and we were just there to drink and smoke marijuana but if he were that nervous we would just leave. I bought a round of drinks for the patrons in the bar and I had my arm around him. I told him that he would have to be a really good shot because he really wasn't but I was. After that he smiled. He said, "You are a crazy white boy". The agent that had been working the area from the beginning said this is crazy; we are going to get shot. He then walked back to the car. I told the black guy we were looking for marijuana and did he know where we could buy some. He told me to go to my car but first buy me a beer. He would then come to my car to meet us. Him and two other black guys came out to the car and he walked up to my car and asked if I had any money. He reached his hand into his sling. At this time the agent who had been there for some time leaned back in the seat because he thought we were about to get shot. The guy asked me what was wrong with him and I told him "Oh he just got finished doing mushrooms, that's why he is acting so scared". The guy pulled out a bag of marijuana and told me it would be $12. The two dollars was for tax. Each one of his buddies pulled out bags and sold them to me. I then asked him if I could sign his sling. I asked for his name and number and wrote it down on a piece of paper so I could contact him if and when I needed more. He said you can come back but don't bring that crazy son-of-a-bitch in the back seat. We left that area and I told my agents to let's get rolling and find more places to buy drugs. After saying that, the first agent again stated that we were crazy and we were going to get killed. I told him he had two choices, "take us to the girl you have been fucking or the only person you made a case on." He took us to the guy's house and he went on to say "he doesn't accept just anyone" I said, "He must, he accepted you". We visited with the guy for about an hour and he proceeded to show us his plants and the plants that were drying for future sales. I asked him if anyone had anything but homegrown and he said only the blacks that he knew of. We left there and went back to our office in Alexandria. The first agent that hadn't got anything accomplished was sent back to that location for another two weeks in which he had done a little better than the time before.

Kentwood

They had sent a partner of mine to Kentwood, LA This was not my assignment but he had been there two weeks and had never made a case. He concocted a scheme to get a brief case and give it to two of Alexandria informants. He told them to meet him at the Sonic Drive-In in Kentwood and act like they were selling him the brief case of drugs in front of the people at the Sonic and also he would look cooler to the locals. How I got involved was the two informants got busted along with the agent and local cops did not want to let them go. The local police didn't believe their story. The police called the Region and I was the one to answer the phone. The police told me what was happening and I assumed it was evidence from our evidence room. Then I explained that they were working undercover. I told him I would drive down and pick up the drugs and show the informants their way back to Alexandria. I was in my car and left town. I left the undercover agent in Kentwood and told him I wouldn't let anyone know what he had done. Before leaving town, ironically I stopped at the Sonic to get something to eat. While there I bought a bag of marijuana from a carhop on skates. I took that bag and threw it in the evidence case because I didn't have the heart to tell on her. I got back to Alexandria along with the informants with no other problems. Nothing would have ever been said except one informant thought he should have had a badge and better police cover. The only thing happened was that nothing was said and the evidence was destroyed.

Lafayette

I officially signed to work Lafayette, LA undercover. I worked three or four weeks. It was one of the most disheartening and disorganized undercover investigations I have ever done. I was supposed to stay on the strip near the college at all times. We tried to meet and talk to numerous people my two weeks there. I said, "I'm tired of being alone" so I went to Alexandria to get two informants to work Lafayette and try to round up drug users. One informant believed to himself that he was a cop. His eyes were always closed while he was talking. The other informant for the sake of no name was called "moomoo". Moomoo's best quality was he never met a stranger and he loved little pony Miller beer. He never had to hold them with his hands as his two top front teeth were missing. Where his two teeth were missing was the perfect spacing for the bottle cap to fit. He would leave it there until he was finished drinking then open another one. I guess he never violated the open container law because it was always in his mouth with it closed. Things got a little better and I made some distribution cases. I guess I made about five cases in a couple days, which isn't too good. The thing that ruined four cases are we all had to stay in a shabby motel and share a van. One guy we had a case on lived next door and while I was sleeping "moomoo" loaned him the state police van. I don't know if any papers were in the van stating whom it belonged to. He came back with the van and it had been ransacked. I kept four evidence bags that was sealed and put in the door panel unseen. He had found the four bags and took them back to his room. Needless to say those cases weren't any good and the guy wouldn't speak to us again. I was pretty mad so we went back to the strip to made more cases. Finally we made a contact with a state police agent girl. Everyone knew she was a cop. She said it was a hard place to work because this particular area was overworked undercover. I thought I had the plague because no one would talk to me. As we were going to the car, we met up with a guy and he was selling ounces of marijuana. He said we were to follow him to his house and each ounce would be $20. The highest we had ever paid. We followed him to his house and I got out the car and followed him to his back door. Once in his house he walked into the other room and came back to where I was and pointed a pistol at me. I told him that I didn't have any money so if you are here to rob me he could have what little I had. His attitude changed then and he pulled out an ounce of marijuana. I paid him $20 and showed him my wallet. He commented that I was a poor son-of-a-bitch like him. Needless to say that was the end of undercover investigation in Lafayette and I was very disappointed because I felt I could have done a better job.

One other thing I had done from Lafayette is I used an informant from Alexandria and he told me to call this guy that he used to buy from him when he needed a large amount of drugs before the holidays. The whole investigation lasted two days and I was badly admonished by my superiors in Alexandria for making cases in another region.

I call the guy with the large amount of drugs from my state police phone line and told him who had given me the information about him. He was a little frightened but he would check on me from the source and he would call me back. I called him back Friday and everything was all right. I told him I wanted sixty pounds of marijuana and he told me he could also get me other drugs. I made the deal and he specifically told me to meet him at the Acadiana Mall and not a minute after or the deal would be off. He said he believed in promptness. He said to me that promptness breeds success. I brought a woman informant with me from Alexandria. She wouldn't know anything about the deal. She went by the nickname of "sweetmeat" if you looked at her you would know why. This was a mistake bringing her because the other agents that I made contact with in Region II made me five minutes late. Instead of concentrating on wiring me they were too busy trying to get wired by "sweetmeat". Every time the agents made a pass at her she would tell them only if her sweet daddy said it was all right. She was referring to me. I was five minutes late and I was standing on the sidewalk of the mall and the guy told me as he pulled up to me that I should not have been late. However, he looked at me and said, "There is no way in the world you could be a cop." He then looked at "sweetmeat" and asked "what about her?" I told him you could be with her after the deal. She will be staying at the mall until the deal is made. He told me to get in the back seat of the car and look at the merchandise and I would show him the money. He had already been followed to where he picked up the drugs from a Tulane professor. The other agents were in different cars and they were supposed to surround his car so he wouldn't drive off. After looking at the drugs I was suppose to throw something out the window, which I did but no one showed up. I still had the window opened and started waving my hand and he said to me "what are you doing". I then told him I was a state police and he was under arrest. He said "there ain't no way man that you are a cop" but when he looked in the back for the money it wasn't there. The other agents forgot the money. They started driving towards us and when he saw them he pulled a gun and starting driving in circles in the mall parking lot and said he would shoot me. Somehow I noticed a machete on the back seat. I picked up the machete and told him if he didn't stop I would chop his damn head off. I reared back like I was about to do it and he immediately stopped the vehicle and started crying. He said why did you do this to me did they have charges on you for you to do this or what. I told him I really was a state police. I don't know who else to tell I am. They arrested him in the parking lot then went on to search his house where he picked the drugs up and the other house at Tulane where he also got drugs. They all stacked the drugs and everyone was laughing and happy and said this was the biggest bust this year and the month was December. I said I had to leave and I would write the report up at my office in Alexandria and mail it to them because I had to leave because the rest of the agents wanted to be with "sweetmeat". I'm not a very fast driver but it took me 3 ½ hours to drive from Lafayette to Alexandria. When I got back to my office they were asking me why didn't I do a bust like that around here. I said I'm a state police and when things come up elsewhere it is my duty to investigate it along with "sweetmeat".

Oakdale

I worked in the town of Oakdale two Friday nights only. I had a lot of dealings in Oakdale after being a policeman but while being a police officer I had to go to a nightclub two consecutive Friday nights. The deal was a state policeman's wife would sneak off to a bar while her husband was in uniform and working the night shift. She got caught and used the excuse to her husband that she was trying to work narcotics. I had to drive there as her boyfriend and go to a dance and let her introduce me to people who were selling drugs. After the second time I had not made any cases except for the one I made on my own. It seemed the moment she got a drink of alcohol she would lose complete control. I had to pack her to the car because she was so drunk and several times during the night I saw her leaving vehicles with different guys. I really don't think she knew what she was doing after drinking for a while and she knew nothing about drugs. I didn't have the heart to tell her husband so I told him she helped lead me into other investigations and I did not need her assistance any longer. I don't know what happened to their marriage but I knew it wasn't going to last.

Natchitoches

One day the captain came in my office and told me he wanted myself and one other to work Natchitoches city. We were supposed to report to the chief of police only and he set us up with an apartment across from the college and by some bars. We didn't have an informant to help us so were were suppose to develop our own leads. The undercover investigation had good promises except that it turned into a four-week party. My partner signed up for college class and we decided to start throwing parties at the apartment. We only invited so many but after a while all sorts of people we didn't invite were showing up. We had people showing up that we had approximately five hundred in a night. They had turned the hole college grounds and complex into a party, in the apartments, on the balconies and on the grounds, stairs and streets. We were getting more famous than some of the fraternities. It was hard to make a case because there were so many people. Several times we made buys and people that were there parting would find the drugs and use them. It seemed like we were furnishing the place, the booze and the drugs. I tried to get away from the apartments and try to go to some bars to meet more people. One night we went to a particular bar and parked in front and we opened the back of our van and was giving out beer to attract people to us. After about one hour at another bar in a shopping center a security guard came up and told us we couldn't sit in the van and drink. At this time we had a few people around us and we were about to make a purchase of drugs. He left and came back with a German shepherd dog on a leash. He again told us to leave and I told him we were not hurting anyone by being there. He then said he would send his attack dog on us if we didn't leave. I said to him "if you send the dog over here I will hit him in the head with a tire tool." I said that in a joking way because I really wasn't trying to cause trouble but I didn't want to leave either. The next thing I know city police arrived and the dog was turned on me and I was arrested for threatening an officer. I couldn't tell them who I was so I had to wait until I got to jail to make a phone call. I used my only phone call and my chief said he would send someone to get me. He took a little longer than I had expected so while I was waiting I was put in a jail cell and immediately got into a fight with another guy in the cell. Every time I was put into a jail cell throughout my career I was always involved in a fight. Before leaving jail I did make friends in the joint and made one distribution case of marijuana in jail. After this happened the captain talked to us again and told me I needed to tone it down because he was getting more complaints on us than anyone else in town. I had to go on my own after this because my partner was going to school. My partner's future wife was also attending at the same time. I couldn't get him to go with me very often so every time I had to make a buy I would go get him so two people would be at the purchase. One night I went on my own to a particular bar that a fraternity was having a big party at. As I got to the door the guy at the door asked for my identification. I showed him the identification and he said I wasn't old enough to go in. I said, "who are you, I am older than you and you are telling me I can't go in?" I walked pass him and he grabbed my arm and swung me around and again stated that I was not going in. He then reared back like he wanted to hit me and I slapped him across his face and he fell to the floor of the bar. Next thing I remembered I was being carried out and punched at the same time by about eight people. They then threw me onto the gravel but luckily for me it was right by my van. They started kicking me and throwing me back and forth as if it were a wrestling match on television. After about five minutes of this I saw my van and luckily I didn't have the door locked. I opened the door and retrieved my pistol from the floorboard. I pulled my pistol on them and they all raided their arms. I said "the next one who hits or kicks me I will shoot their ass off." I made everyone of them lie on the ground. I got in my van and drove away. The only thing I took from them was a belt from one of their hands that they had used to whip me. I got back to the apartment and I was too beat up to go anywhere else. I didn't feel like making any more cases so I stayed away for a couple days at the apartment. After that my partner decided to work with me a little but we still didn't do much good without causing so much trouble.

The next time I was in trouble there I bought some drugs from this one guy who wanted me to drive him to work because he had left his keys. We drove him to the Army surplus store that he said he worked at. We waited in the van while he went around the side then came around to open the door for us. We were all in the building and he wanted us to look around and get anything we wanted. The next thing we remember was the police showing up and we were arrested for burglary and drug possession. We found out that the guy didn't work there he just used us for the ride over there so he could break into the place. Again we were brought to jail and again I had to make a phone call so we could be bailed out. The guy that broke into the place convinced the other officers that arrested us that we held a gun to him and demanded him to rob the place. He also made a statement that we enticed him to do it for drugs. He made his long statement and signed it. We didn't have a statement we only had a phone call. Needless to say they were very embarrassed after they found out what the real deal was. They had to go and arrest the guy again. We knew we couldn't stay there much longer because the other police were finding out who were. We stayed one more night there and our captain told us to call it off. We went back to the apartment to gather our things and some college students showed up, then more came and even more and once again we had a huge party going on. There were a lot of people there at the beginning strip dancing. About ten different girls took off all their clothes. All the men from the apartment complex were to judge them on performance, body content, and ability. One college girl after another would jump on the table and dance. A lot of guys sat around a table and watched. What I was worried about was two of the girls that were dancing knew I was a state policeman from Jonesboro. Everyone was getting drunk and loud and after the girls would finish dancing they would fall into the guy that they wanted to be with. My partner and I made sure that the two girls from Jonesboro fell off the table into our arms that way they would be quite. After all the music and dancing here came the police again. We were charged with disturbing the peace, public ludeness, and possession of firearms. I had two pistols on me, one on my waste and one in my boot. As we were leaving the apartment the chief radioed the officers who were bringing me to jail and asked if it was my apartment where the commotion was going on. They told him yes and they were instructed to drive my partner, the girls and myself back to my apartment so they could get dressed and said that our apartment was being condemned. We got back to our office in Alexandria and the captain was waiting for us. He said something like crime had went down fifty percent while we were there.

As far as working Natchitoches it was more or less a waste of time and money. We did try one more investigation there. We had arrested this guy in Alexandria before and he said he would help us by introducing me to some people in Natchitoches. I can say this, he was very gay. We were invited to his parties in Natchitoches and he would introduce us around so we could buy pills and marijuana. My partner had to act like he was his date for the night. We got to the party and everyone was dressed in costumes. My partner put a dog collar around his neck and figured that would make him fit in better. After about thirty minutes at the party we just sat there. We were too scared to socialize. Everyone in the house got completely naked including the boy's mom and sister. They were all running around the house with a hard on and we waited by the back door so we would be able to make a quick run. I grabbed the informant by the hair and dragged him to the curb while he was buck-naked with a hard on. I told him we are here to buy drugs from one person and if he didn't straighten up I would drag his ass across the pavement. He said, "O.K. big boy I'm ready" I called him a crazy son of a bitch and we left as soon as we could. The informant had small electrical wires hooked to his nuts. My partner took his dog collar off and starting beating the shit out of the informant with it and all he accomplished was keeping the informant with a hard on.

This was the second time this happened with this informant so we never used him again. All in all we did not make many cases in Natchitoches because of the distance and the locals had it in control. These undercover investigations were not in order. I just remembered what happened with each investigation I was involved in.

Marksville

One day the sergeant came to me and asked me if I would go to all the local pharmacies and go to the back and give them the order of drugs that I wanted. I didn't want to do it because I knew they wouldn't sell me anything because of the way I looked. I went to seven different pharmacies and asked for a painkiller and a speed pill. Most of them would ask how many I wanted and would sell to me over the counter without a prescription. These were all down town Marksville pharmacies. The first six I went to were not very new pharmacist and they never had problems selling to me because they wanted to hurry and get me out of their store. The last pharmacy I went to, which was pharmacy number seven, I walked to the back where the pharmacist was and told him the same line and told him exactly what I wanted. I told him I didn't have a written prescription but I would get him one if he wanted me to. He said "no problem, go up to the front of the store and wait until I bring the prescription to you." He said it didn't look good for his business to have me in there looking trashy and smelling bad. After he walked up and gave me my prescription, I took four steps out the store and two sheriff's department cars from Avoyelles Parish pulled their guns and told me to hit the ground. They handcuffed me and charged me with drug possession and possession of a firearm. I had more than that but I saw the deputies taking the pills as we were in the parking lot. I told them I had walked to the pharmacy because I didn't want them searching my car and taking more drugs for themselves. They took me to the jail and threw me in the third story of the jail with no phone call. The third floor jail cells were not air-conditioned. They used a huge fan like you would see in an auto mechanic shop. Not even two minutes after I was there one inmate starting fighting with me. They tried to push me into the fan. They wanted to see how bad it would chop me up. Just before being pushed into the fan I pulled the pistol from my boot that the police didn't find when they had searched me. I made them all sit on the floor with their legs crossed and arms in the air. I stayed in jail for three hours before the sheriff of Avoyelles took me from the jail cell and into his office. The sheriff said he found out who I was and he was sorry for the inconvenience and gave me back my pistol and switchblade knife that I had in my boot. I showed him the other pistol I had in my other boot while in jail to protect myself. The sheriff was a strong political figure in the state because he was the only sheriff that was elected while he was in jail serving time. He told me to walk back to my car and I had better notify him before I do any narcotic investigations in his parish. He also said the cases that I had previously made had better be thrown away. Not believing him, I thought surely the state police was bigger than a sheriff but when I got back to my office I was told I should not have gotten caught and do not write any reports on cases I had made. They said if anyone could do it they believed I would be the one to go in there and not get caught. They went on to tell me that I should have spent more time in jail maybe it would have taught me a lesson. They took all the evidence and dumped it in a jar with others and threw all the individual bottles away. We kept the pickle jar in the office and over time it was completely filled.

I had one other time to work in Marksville on the outskirts of Avoyelles Parish. A local narcotic agent for the parish needed a state policeman to assist him with a search warrant in Effie, LA. It was an ongoing feud between this agent and the defendant he was after. What started that day was the local agent passed the defendant and when doing so the defendant shot the agent the bird. The agent got back to his office and was really mad. He said "I can make up enough probable cause to get a search warrant" that was to get the judge to sign it. We were called at the state police office to assist him after we thought he had secured a valid search warrant. My sergeant and I and other officers followed him to the defendant's house and started serving the search warrant. We searched the house every which way you could and a number of green houses he had. The defendant's wife had a lot of legal potted houseplants in the green houses. Just before the search ended the agent was getting very upset because he couldn't find anything. I told him we needed to get on out of there because the marijuana wasn't there and that maybe they would come back another day when it would be. Before leaving, being upset as this agent was along with my sergeant, they took two cans of WD40 and sprayed all the hundreds of houseplants that were in the green houses. They just kept saying to me don't tell anyone. I told them I would not take part in this. The agent that had the search warrant broke everything that he could and was going to put drugs in the defendant's house. I told him I have seen you do this before and I refuse to be a part. I am leaving. Things like this were really beginning to take a mental toll on my competence as a state policeman.

We didn't arrest anyone except the guy that gave the finger to the agent but it wasn't for drugs. Not finding any drugs they charged him with reveling an officer. Which simply meant the agent was mad that he shot him the finger.

One a Thursday afternoon the captain came to me and wanted me to run an undercover investigation in Northeast parishes of Louisiana dealing with gambling. I asked him what kind of gambling that it was illegal everywhere in the state. I told him you know the last time we investigated any kind of gambling the guy was fired and one was made to retire. He promised me it would not be like this. He told me to hit the towns of Newellton, Tallulah, Lake Providence and other small towns in the area. We started in Ferriday and wound up in Natchez, Mississippi. By the time we were through we had played black jack, slot machines, dice, roulette and any other games of chance. We had lost over $2000.00 that night at the different places. As per instructions to spend as much as we wanted. At this time gambling was illegal in the state, however, all these small parishes allowed the gambling to keep going in bars. I would say that Tallulah was the worst. Most of the gambling was in black bars. You had to be a member to play in the white bars. We came back after doing this for one night and the captain said we didn't have to do this any longer. We wrote our reports condemning numerous bars of gambling, under age drinking and prostitution. After writing our reports we never heard anything about the cases we made. It was about twenty years after this that gambling was legal in the state. The way I figured someone told someone to leave the gambling establishments alone.

Baker

I knew I would be assigned to work somewhere in the Baton Rouge area because of the State Police Annual Convention. Once a year members of the state police get together for the annual convention. They pick different cities in the state to have the convention. I went to the convention only once in my career. It was in Houma, Louisiana. The convention was for anybody in the state police, detectives or uniform. I met the people that ran the state police narcotics office from Baton Rouge at the convention. They continuously asked me to work undercover as a narcotics officer in Baton Rouge. They were in need of my services and I wound up working twice for them. The first time was approximately two months and the second only took two weekends. The first investigation I was stationed to work undercover in Baker, Louisiana. This town was about five or ten miles Northeast of Baton Rouge. It seemed like it was part of Baton Rouge because everything was so close together. One big distinction to get to

Baker from Baton Rouge was that you had to drive through Scottlandville, which are ninety-nine percent niggers.

I lived with this guy and his wife in a trailer park. They had to make room for me to sleep. He told everyone in the area that I was his friend from Angola State Prison. He had been in prison prior narcotics arrest. He and I got along well because by this time my impression of state police was very complicated. By this I meant that I didn't see any end to the way of winning any type of drug war. The police, I felt, was some of the problem and not the answer but this was my job so I did it to the best of my ability.

This investigation had "success" written all over it. From start to finish, I was making drug deals. I met people and tried to make most of my deals in Baker because of the chief of police was putting out most of the money. I made about one hundred different cases give or take a few and I bought a multitude of drugs except heroine. I could have bought that particular drug but I was getting too deep with the niggers in Scottlandville and Baton Rouge with heroine. I observed heroine being delivered once while I was standing on the street with thirty other niggers in Scottlandville. I made a few cases in Scottlandville from the niggers because they wanted me to be down on the corner with them. The guy I was staying with did not want to stay there; he would drop me off only to pick me up in a couple of hours. A normal look when working in Scottlandville would be thirty to forty niggers and myself standing on the corner street waiting for white LSU college students to come by and purchase any assortment of drugs. The advantage of me being there was the white kids would not be as scared to stop and buy something. What I'd have to do is when they stopped, the niggers wanted to walk out to the car and greet the kids. Generally, the guys in the cars would tell me what kind of drugs they wanted. I would have to convey what they wanted to the guys on the sidewalk. They thought that would conceal their identity and the kind of drugs that the people wanted. I would never handle the drugs; the person who was selling the drug would come out and talk to them while I stood there. I would make a case by this example, if they sold marijuana or pills I would ask the nigger "where's my cut?" instead of them giving me money they would give me drugs as payment. After I felt that I had distribution on the main ones I had to quit going to Scottlandville. The policemen in Scottlandville had gotten word that a white person was hanging on the corner. Often when the Scottlandville City Police would come by the black dealers on the street would hide me near the corners of buildings or cover me up some kind of way so the police couldn't see me at night. Sometimes I had to sit in their cars and lay down so the police couldn't see me. The police told them that they were looking for me because of my status in the drug dealership. All this did was tip off the dealers that it was an informant in the group and they wanted me to help them look for him. This also made me feel that I needed to get out of Scottlandville. So I concentrated more on Baker where I was suppose to.

In an investigation like this it would always lead to bigger fish. I found myself meeting people in Baton Rouge or going there. I made one deal in Baker for cocaine and if I wanted to buy anymore he would introduce me to his Baton Rouge connection. I remember going to Baton Rouge and meeting an LSU football player who said he played linebacker. I bought a little bit from him and made a bigger deal to make a later purchase. I showed up that night to make my purchase and they had already typed a search warrant for the linebacker's apartment. I had a wire on underneath my shirt and it would record the conversation we had. There was a certain word I was suppose to use when I saw the cocaine then the police would raid the apartment. The taped wire was uncomfortable so I moved it. This saved me because he looked for it on my chest. After getting to his apartment he took me to a back room with a freezer in it. He being about 6'4" and not fat at all I was kind of scared when he double locked the door. He showed me the cocaine and I gave the code however he didn't here what was going on in the rest of the apartment. Instead of pulling out the money I took out my gun and told him I was a state policeman and he was under arrest. He didn't believe me the first time and looked as if he was going to jump at me. Again I said you are under arrest and he froze looking at me. I finally told him again you hear the noise in the other rooms I said this is it you get down on the floor or I am going to shoot you. He looked at me shaking and you would believe what happened next. He stared urinating on himself and then laid down in it. I told him to stay still and then opened the door for the other cops to take him away.

Another thing that stood out is that when I purchased some regular pain pills from this young fellow he said he would get me more from his friend's house. I went with him and met his friend who had broke into seventeen drug stores. He had every kind of pill in quantities you wanted. I purchased some and told him I would be back for more. The officer ran a search warrant on this also however, the guy was still together enough to get his tackle box of pills and hide it in the woods. When I went back he told me that the police came by and didn't find it. I told him to hide it where it wouldn't get wet. He said he didn't and asked me if I could help him hide it better. We went and got the two boxes and I told him to give them to me and I would hide them. He said he had a place and would not let me have them. Well by seeing his size and it was no way I was going to let him keep all of those drugs I had to do something. I turned him around and hit him straight in the nose knocking him out. I grabbed the drugs and drove to a secluded place and burned all of them. This officer I was working with did not want to take time out to help me so I had to do it alone.

Another purchase I made was from a young guy who was selling marijuana in Baker. We drove to his house and he took us to his back yard. I told him I wanted just a couple of ounces. He raised up a piece of tin where he had hidden the marijuana. He reached his hand under the tin, got me the marijuana and as he was putting the tin back down to cover the rest of his supply he was bitten on the hand by a rattle snake. He pulled his hand back real fast and the snake was still hanging on. He ran to his house and one of his parents immediately took him to the hospital.

I had made a number of drug purchases in Baker that all led to bigger buys of drugs but I had to stop because of the money supply. The chief of police in Baker wanted only numbers, which I assumed was for political reasons. The informant I was working with seemed to know a lot of people, which helped me make a lot of cases. He had been in Angola previously and he didn't want to go back. I think he tried to do a really good job, which led to a lot of cases. One time as we were in down town Baton Rouge a black subject wanted to sell us some pills. He was giving us a hard time and I thought we would be robbed until he saw a cross earring that the informant wore which meant he was from Angola. After so many weeks of working and being away from home I was getting very run down and ready to go home. The office in Baton Rouge had a round up of everyone I had bought drugs from and they filled the jail in Baker. After all were arrested, they wanted me to walk down the hall in front of the jail cells and show everyone my badge. I think this had an effect on the defendants.

I had worked in West Baton Rouge and this was the only time I had testified because they really wanted to close this one bar because they were violating all the laws. The Baton Rouge police wanted me to make a narcotics distribution case so I brought an informant "sweetmeat" with me. She could get in with the guys a lot easier so we found marijuana from one guy a the bar and he turned out to be an undercover narcotics state policeman. Finally we found someone else with marijuana and he wanted us to go to his car and smoke a joint with him. After a little while in the car we encouraged him to bring some of the joints into the bar so we could smoke it and he did. He lit a joint in the bar and I kept it for evidence, which made the owner of the bar responsible. I had to testify at a hearing to have his license revoked and they were.

Lake Charles

My last official undercover case was in Lake Charles and I can say it lasted longer than any of the other cases keep in mind while I worked undercover I came back to my home office in Alexandria and worked undercover here also. This undercover was ran by the same people that set up the Baker undercover cases. It was well put together and I had a very good informant to work with. The only trouble is I had to live with her in her house, which was a very old house. I had a room to myself at night when I wasn't busy making cases. I had to keep my door locked. The investigation started o.k. and I told her what I wanted done and get it over as soon as possible. This was impossible to do because I make over one hundred cases in a week and a half. I had a very fancy car which was a Trans Am heavily souped up. After about four days of staying at her house she invited two more girls to live in the house with us. They were both prostitutes and they wanted me to pimp them. I told them I was a detective and they could have all the money they made. They said I was the best pimp they ever had. One girl was a Mexican and rated on the scale as an eight and the other girl was white and on the scale as a seven. She was new into the racket. The Mexican girl's husband used to be a pimp and he was now in jail. I talked to him one time on the phone and he said he would kill me when he got out of jail. She told him she would be with me only. It seemed to be a good cover and I played the part. The worse thing about it was they thought I was very crazy and gay. They wanted to sleep with me at night and I had to keep my door locked. They kept me awake because they stayed up all night. One time I shot a hole in the ceiling to make them shut up. I had distribution cases on both the girls. The golden rule was if you fuck'em you can't bust'em. As far as the girl that I was originally working with there was no problem as she weighted about four hundred pounds. We lived in an apartment in Westlake and we were all partying and were the terror of the neighborhood. To keep them happy I would have to drive them to car auctions at a motel so they could turn tricks. I would have to watch the room because if there were trouble they would switch the light on and off. I made a lot of cases with people that they went to bed with. I eventually met everyone I could in Westlake that was involved with drugs. It was very easy to buy drugs because I believe most of the people there thought they were like the people from Orange, Texas.

Like all undercover investigations everyone could say they made buys. One buy that I was proud of was this black pimp. He was upset that I was doing business without notifying him. He went by the nickname "Drum". He met me at a parking lot by a phone and I didn't know what he was up to. Come to find out he wanted me to fix him up with my two pretty girls for the next night and for two hours. I told him that I didn't know if I could arrange this and I wanted to know what was in it for me. He brought preludes to sell to me, which was a scheduled narcotic. He said they are in the pay phone change holder. I really thought he would shoot me in the back as I went to get the pills but the pills were there and I retrieved them and paid him for them. I convinced the girls to go and see him the next day. When the girls came back they were fussing at me saying they didn't want to be with that old nigger man anymore. On a normal car auction night the girls could make any where from $500 - $1000. It was a constant fight to keep them off me. I mostly spent my time on the front porch playing solitaire. The only thing that I did do was they wanted to see my dick. I showed it to them. I asked them "are you satisfied because that is as close as you will get to it." As I stayed there I made a lot of buys. I was really burnt out working undercover. It was hard to distinguish myself from the drug attics. I had to smoke marijuana on several occasions and I didn't have anyone to report to because it was a two-man office. One agent was frightened of his own shadow and the other agent stayed at parties in Baton Rouge at the governor's mansion. I started slipping into the people that used drugs. I was told to go to this apartment in Westlake and a guy that I had purchased from earlier would be there. I would buy more speed from him. When I got to the apartment the lights were out and I knew they were there and something didn't seem right. As soon as I knocked on the door two people pulled me into the apartment immediately. I started fighting with them trying to get loose while one guy was filling a syringe with urine. I broke loose and jumped through the window and dropped to the ground and took off in my car. I don't know why they were after me but they thought that I stole some of their drugs the night before. I did meet the people at a house in Lake Charles but I could not talk to anyone, as they were all semi conscious because of drug abuse. The biggest advantage I had in Lake

Charles as I was always riding in a Trans Am that went very fast. I usually had a number of good-looking prostitutes with me. It was hard to report to anyone because frankly I think they thought of me as complete trash and wanted to use me just to verify the office in Lake Charles. I made a lot of cases and I averaged around five or six cases per day on distribution charges. Some times it would take me a whole day to write up different cases. At this time I was also working on a deal from Houston, Texas from my home office and was working with a Rapides Parish deputy because I could trust him. I begged him to wait on that deal until I got through with Lake Charles. Lake Charles undercover investigation was mostly centered in Westlake and it turned into a life of its own. I was very frustrated and didn't want to go on but they said I was doing so well and that I needed to stay with it. I made cases from about anybody that sold drugs around this area. I even bought marijuana from a priest on the promise that I would come back and visit him later in the night. I don't remember who the priest was but all I wanted to do is get back the drugs to him and tell him I wasn't interested. As you can see raised as a catholic how disoriented I had become. The very nature of the undercover investigation made me become very hated by the local officers because they knew who I was. Every night before returning to the apartment very late you could see the local police in marked cars waiting on the out skirts of the city limits. As soon as I would see them I would gun my car and be at my apartment about one mile away in no time. They didn't have a chance of catching me because of how fast my car would travel. They would pull to the apartment as I got there and I would already be inside my apartment. They would never stop after I was already in the apartment but one day I was playing cards on the porch and they pulled up there to question me and ask if they could come inside my apartment. I told them if they didn't have a search warrant that they had better not come back. There were about three older cops and one said we really just want to talk to you. Two of the officers grabbed me while they beat me up and threw me off the porch. They told me if they caught me the right way this beaten was nothing compared to what they would really do to me.

Towards the end of this undercover investigation the agent wanted to come to Lake Charles and pick me up to work on the Houston deal. I will discuss this in a later chapter. I feel by me going along with him, local Alexandria police and total lies by my fellow state police officers led to me being fired. I didn't need to leave Lake Charles when I did because I was working on a lab. A guy and two girls that had completely see through blouses wanted to set up a lab in the apartment I was staying at. We had already had enough trouble with the landlord because of how filthy the apartment was with busted pipes and needles lying everywhere. He wanted to evict us but one of the girls had taken down his pants and gave him a blowjob so he wouldn't do anything to us. In closing the Lake Charles investigation showed me just how bias narcotics arrest were. They kept stressing the fact for me to make more cases on black people. In Westlake this was a problem. The undercover case ended as I was terminated from the state police.

Alexandria

My main office was centered in Alexandria and after so many months everyone knew who I was so I had to work with informants.

I said earlier in the book we had no funds to work with in Alexandria but later on I started getting my share of funds. We had an interim sergeant until someone took the exam to be a sergeant in narcotics. The interim sergeant was a drunk and totally worried about what myself and my friend could get into. One morning we played a joke on the sergeant by telling him we pulled over a car but didn't find any drugs. We had to help them push the car off to get it started and it happened to be on the levy. I told the sergeant we lost control of the car and it ran into the river. He threatened to lock us in a closet so we wouldn't go out at night and mess up any more. My partner had the nickname of "Wrong Address Mister Search Warrant" We had a search warrant of a house but had the wrong address and we searched it thinking this was the correct house and found a lot of marijuana in it. We also searched the correct house and it contained drugs also. The biggest problem was if you arrested the wrong people ninety-eight percent of the time they wanted to help us bust someone else.

One of the first things I saw that I didn't like, my partner had a vehicle accident and he was to say it wasn't his fault by his supervisor. I could see what they wanted him to do so in gaining their trust I immediately agreed with them. After that they said, "He must be like us." The majority of policemen that I ran into believed the laws were not made for them but for the officers to enforce them.

The reason he had the accident was that he was so excited about possible having our first search warrant. Up to this point we had just made some buys only and we never worked as informants for a search warrant. We met with the informant and he told us where a large quantity of pharmaceutical drugs were. They had a large number of drug store burglaries in Rapides Parish area that n one was able to solve. He took us to the house where he had seen a lot of drugs so we sent him in to buy some. He then took us to a house in the out of town area and said there were a lot of drugs in that house but he didn't see any drugs in the second. According to the rules of search and seizure he had satisfied the reason to search the first house but not the second. We typed up the search warrant for the first house and got it signed and it was perfectly legal, however we searched the first house and found enough drugs to fill three pharmacies. As we entered the house a drug dealer was shooting up morphine. This caught the attention of the newspaper and all the locals. My partner and I thought since he was right on the first house but still not seeing anything in the second house we lied on the search warrant. We searched the second house, which belonged to a dealer's grandmother, and this house was full of drugs also. The next day the defendant's and a team of the most prominent lawyers showed up at our office quickly learned that the ends never justify the means. Our government today sort of works like that by making up stuff. On a good weekend I would run anywhere from two to five search warrants. I never had another bad search warrant after that except when an informant brought the drugs to someone's house and then told me that they were there. This I consider one of the lowest forms of police work. In between undercover agents while I was out of town I would call in other agents to cover for me. I brought one agent from Shreveport and he turned out to be a common drunk and I had to send him back home. I brought another agent from Lafayette and he was scared to death. I brought a female agent in and I put her with one of the best informants possible. She was invited to go to a dogfight her first weekend here. By Monday several people knew she was a narcotics agent already because of the pistol in her purse and her badge. Someone had looked inside her purse while she was unaware. No one hurt her in any way. After that she made one case and it was never prosecuted because I think she went to bed with him. I brought a black agent in and we sent him down one street with an informant and he walked along the walls of the buildings as if he would be stabbed at any minute he did this for about three blocks so we picked him up and brought him back to his hotel. He begged for us to let him go because he wasn't cut out for this type work. We allowed him to leave and go to him hometown.

When I was in the Alexandria office I worked closely with city parish narcotics agents for Rapides Parish. They were angry with me on a regular basis because their informants would call me when they wouldn't answer their phones. Most of them stayed drunk and played cards all night. I only attended one party they had and it was on Cane River. This sticks out in my mind because we would chase each other with boats and try to run over skiers. We had one big bass boat that would pull the skier and a small aluminum boat to chase. We had a bass boat but this boat was only used to pick up the skiers. The man driving the small aluminum boat would come up and cut the rope of the skier and we were all drunk. I was in the chase boat for a short while then I cut the rope and heard the skier's head hit the boat. The point of this story is as I drove to the bank there was a black guy sitting on the bank smoking marijuana. I asked him if I could have a joint and he said "sure". I told him my buddies might want some too and how much are you charging for it. I brought all my buddies to the bank while the black guy was fishing. We stayed in our boats. All at one time we looked at him and pulled out our badges. He threw his pole in the water and ran up the bank as fast as he could. It looked like a scene from the little rascals. We never did arrest him as we were laughing so hard and couldn't stop.

The deal was we were suppose to work with Metro narcotics but the old saying was tell them as little as possible because we were working for the state and we felt above them. The feds treated us the same way. We worked our own investigations unless they needed our help. I worked more with Metro than any other. I didn't trust them but I had to show them how to do search warrants. Everyone that has done search warrants I will high light the better ones. One investigation was to arrest a guy who was bringing in a large amount of marijuana. We had a whole lot of people working on this particular case and I had my sergeant with me in the car. I instructed everyone that I wanted to be there when it was going down. I was driving down a four lane and a lady turned left in front of me. She was knocked unconscious along with my sergeant. My sergeant was new with narcotics so he liked to work along with me. I woke him up and we borrowed a civilian's car and went to the arrest scene. We eventually arrested the guy with twenty-eight pounds of marijuana. It was hard working with the other agencies because they were doing a lot of things I didn't approve of. I drove up to one scene that was a burglary and a uniformed policeman was loading television sets and putting them in his car. One officer asked me what was I doing there and I didn't respond I just left. Another time was when they helped me arrest a black guy and took him to the city jail. He had given us a little hassle and it irritated the uniformed policeman a lot more. Two officers brought him up in the elevator. I told them I didn't want to go up in the elevator I would take the stairs. When I met them at the jail they had beaten up the black subject pretty bad.

I went on another search warrant with an agent in a motel room and we searched the room completely and found nothing. The next thing I knew the agent that had the search warrant had an ounce of marijuana with him. He put the marijuana in the sofa cushion after which I told him I didn't want anything to do with him. He and his team eventually arrested a guy with that ounce of marijuana. I had another more warrant that a couple was due into town with a whole lot of marijuana in a particular car. I gave this information to a young police officer and I told him to handle it and also told him we didn't have enough information to stop the vehicle immediately. The car showed up at about 2:30 p.m. and we pulled them over. I told the officer to get a search warrant since we had the information confirmed. Instead he got so excited he opened the trunk and found a large amount of marijuana. We lost the case in court because of his testimony.

I went on a joint search warrant in Alexandria and the Assistant District Attorney wanted to come along. The Assistant District Attorney got there before we did and he was drunk. When we entered the house the Assistant District Attorney was sitting on the couch visiting with the homeowners. He told everyone who he was and my sergeant told me to drive him home because he was so drunk.

I had another search warrant in Pineville, which led to the arrest of thirty-two people. We had to use a paddy wagon to bring them all to jail. Some of the people I had arrested two or three times previously. The only comment made was don't fill up the jail this weekend we don't have any more room.

Another search warrant was when an informant I had drove to Houston to see someone he knew that was selling drugs. After he got there they came back to Alexandria to meet us on the pretense of trading marijuana for pharmaceutical Quaaludes. My sergeant worked out a deal with a wholesale drug company to get sealed Quaalude bottles so we could show them so they would bring the marijuana. We met with them in a motel and they brought some marijuana with them and they in turn wanted to see the Quaaludes. They had about one ounce of marijuana with them and they wanted us to smoke it to see how good it was. All the agents looked at me and told me to smoke it. I asked them why I had to. After doing that I was pretty messed up. The dealers insisted on a sample of Quaaludes. We knew we couldn't give them a sample because it would mess up the case. My sergeant busted one of the bottles open and gave them a Quaalude. I knew right then the case was over. We had just done what they had done. They wanted us to write a report and lie about giving out the Quaalude but

I told them I wasn't going to. They showed up about three days later at an informant's house and they had about sixty-five pounds of marijuana. We were wired and were to get a signal when the other officers hit the place to arrest them. They were all armed and the one closest to me had something similar to a machine gun. We took a package of marijuana to cut in sections to be weighed and the signal was given. The guy closest to me I raised his arm up slowly and put a pistol in his armpit. I told him I was crazy and I didn't mind shooting him right there. He was very frightened because of how I looked and threw his gun on the ground. It was a big arrest quantity wise but we had to drop the charges because of what my sergeant did.

Another occasion was that I had just arrested an individual and booked him in the jail when I received a call from another city for help. The agent was a friend of mine and we called him "Stems" because every search warrant that he had resulted in just finding marijuana stems which wasn't against the law. I immediately left the courthouse and ran a stop sign on my way to Pineville. I looked behind me and saw a car following me. I made a turn in Pineville to see if the car would follow me, which he did. I stopped immediately and jumped from my car with my gun pulled. I recognized the guy because he was the Mayor of Pineville. He said I didn't need my gun in his city. I asked him "if that's you Mayor what is the problem"? He said he observed me running a stop sign in Alexandria and speeding in Pineville and he had his girlfriend in his car as a witness. He told me I was under arrest and I was to go with him. I told him that he couldn't arrest me for a misdemeanor and that he had no authority to play policeman. I said I was going to your station to help somebody but now I'm going home. After about ten minutes of being home he sent two officers to my house. I knew the officers and they told me that he was fussing at headquarters and told them it was now time to get the longhaired narcotics officers off the street. They knew that they couldn't do anything to me so they sat at my kitchen table and said they would wait around until the Mayor cooled off before they went back to the office. I had forgotten about all this until I went to the office the next morning. I was told, by my sergeant and the Regions III Commander, to call the Mayor and apologize. I said no way will I call him after which the Region III Commander gave me special duties for about two weeks. He had me watching different people in his church to see who was going out on whom. I was working domestic cases. He never liked me saying my hair was too long and I looked trashy and he didn't want to associate with me.

I will fill in a few cases of narcotics that I thought were interesting. One search warrant, and I arrested this subject that I was told to drop the charges on this subject immediately. I couldn't use him any longer. I told the District Attorney I couldn't use him any longer. I told him this was the exact reason nothing was getting done. I had listened to him and he said a few things to me that weren't polite and I looked at him and told him to go to hell. We all secretly used this informant even though the District Attorney was against this. I remember one time the informant came to the office and he had six ounces of marijuana with him. He told us were he bought it from and he asked us to reimburse him. We didn't have the money to pay him back because the District Attorney's office ran out of funds for the month. My sergeant told the informant to take the marijuana back and try to sell it elsewhere to get his money back because we couldn't pay him. We found out where he bought it and ran a search warrant and found the marijuana that the informant sold back earlier. I told them that I didn't need to run this search warrant and another agent with me said he was going through with it. I told them I thought it was entrapment and I would not testify.

Another search warrant was with the Air Force. I had worked with them previously along with OSI undercover at the now closed England Airpark. I had gotten a tip from a reliable informant at least three airmen living in a house off base and had a large amount of marijuana in a trunk under the house. I already knew where the marijuana was stored but I couldn't go straight to it or it would have burned my informant. There were several agents from OSI and one from another parish and then some from Metro and the rest were state police. When we hit the house there were several people in the house. Three Air Force guys, one being my distant cousin, which was a surprise and three naked women. I was rounding them up to sit in the living room and I told OSI and the other agents don't find anything because they weren't from this area and they would not be able to testify. Two girls got dressed right away and we placed them all under arrest before we found anything. It was my belief that if you had enough evidence to search you should have enough evidence to arrest. The one girl left was still asleep in the bedroom. I knocked on the door and she said for me to come in and she was completely naked. I told her who I was and she said I could have sex with her first before she had to get dressed. I told her to get dressed and get moving. Instead of searching and having an agent to assist OSI, everyone wanted to see the naked woman. I then heard someone holler outside the house saying he found something. I walked outside and told him he didn't find shit and for him to go inside and watch the prisoners. He was shaking he was so happy he found something. I called another agent and told him to look under the house and he did find the trunk and I told him to pull it out. It was an Air Force trunk with about thirty-five pounds of marijuana. The informant I used on this case was one of my best and most reliable. I got in trouble for paying him too much for his information.

All I can say was it was a constant battle of who was going to do what. No one trusted one another. I was always getting into trouble working with Metro narcotics too much. I wanted to transfer out of narcotics but hey would not allow me to because there was no one to take my place. My partner was transferred. They wanted me to stay and be a sergeant. They didn't' know how sick I was of this lifestyle.

Another case I had and with a new partner was a gun nut. He liked to play with his gun and spin it around loaded and unloaded. I had to set with him for three days at the Esler Field Airport in the private section because we had information that a subject was in his own plane was flying in from Houston and loaded with drugs. Now in order to get a search warrant for an airplane you had to go the District Attorney personally and he would help you in writing the search warrant and get a Judge to sign it. This subject was from a wealthy family. His dad owned several factories and other places in the local area and not thinking I knew I messed up because I knew someone would tell his dad we were waiting for him at the airport. We sat there for three days around the clock waiting for him to land. I got so aggravated with my partner playing with his gun so I took it from him and locked it in the trunk. I told him he was very obnoxious and I would give it back to him when he needed it. I received a call to call the informant and he told me the guy had already came in with a large amount of cocaine and hash and landed at a remote airport in the area. The next day the guy that had the drugs and the plane phoned us and said he wanted to meet with us. He told us that we could never bust him because he would know about it right away and that someone had informed his dad that we were waiting for him. This is what made me want to leave narcotics. We knew it was the District Attorney or the Judge that told his dad. I was sick of drunk Assistant District Attorneys and sick of people asking me to fix tickets and very sick of drunk ass Judges.

One occasion that comes to mind is I was invited to go to a private hunting club to shoot ducks with my sergeant a local Judge and the sheriff. The Judge and Sheriff was drunk off their ass. The man that owned the place was a Federal Magistrate. He handled all game violations. He owned his own hunting club near the river. Everyone was interested in hunting there. He took us into pits of water where wood ducks would come to roost. They would come in so fast that my sergeant and I kept shooting. The limit on wood ducks at the time was two per person. We killed well over sixty between the two of us. The barrel of my gun was so hot and I had to reload so fast that I put a shell in backwards so I had to quit shooting. He had to bring us out to the sight in his four-wheel drive vehicle so he returned to pick us up close to dark. He said, "Y'all had a good hunt Huh? Y'all killed all these birds by yourself?" We loaded up fifty-six ducks in grass sacks and went to get the Sheriff. When we got to the Sheriff he was drunk and had fallen to the ground. His gun was stuck in the mud and he couldn't shoot. The Judge had run off the road and buried his vehicle half way in the mud. He was pretty drunk and could barely make it to the hunting lodge. The lodge was two stories and very nice. When we got to the lodge he offered us a drink and said we would get two niggers to clean our ducks so we wouldn't have to. We were all sitting around in the lodge and the Judge asked me if I like coming out there. I told him I liked the part where you could kill as many ducks as you wanted. He asked me if I wanted to come back and I could but he had a proposition for me. He gave me the name of his alleged secretary and wanted me to find out if she used drugs or anything else that might be in her background. I said to him, "you mean I have to find out something on her before I can come back?" He said "Well you don't get something for nothing." I got mad and I told him it wasn't worth me coming out here and being bribed just so he could keep fucking his secretary so his wife wouldn't find out. He said he didn't want to loose his reputation if she was mixed up in something. I told him he could kiss my ass and I never want to come here again and give the ducks to your nigger that was suppose to clean them. My sergeant got upset that he asked me that but he was also upset with me for saying that to the judge. I said I didn't need a friend like him so on the way out the Judge had left before we did and we found him stuck in the ditch. We offered him a ride home but he said he would get himself home.

Judges would sign search warrants for me because they knew that I would not go on bad information. The ends never justified the means. One night I had to go to a judge to sign a search warrant and he was so drunk he didn't know what he was signing. We ran a search warrant on a trailer for a second time and I had myself, an agent, and two uniform police to go with me. I knew the people in the trailer so I knocked and told them I'm back and to open the door. I told the uniform police to get his gun out and that this would be easy. He pulled his gun and started charging towards the door and his gun went off. About the same time the one I sent around back of the trailer fired a warning shot, which was a no-no. After arresting this subject for a second time I knew him pretty good. The troop already heard about a gun being fired. I went to the two state policeman and they hadn't been on the job very long. I told them I would write the report and say that I was the one doing the shooting.

The Air Force people seemed to be the easiest to bust because they wanted to make friends on the outside and if they got in trouble they would tell on them first. I would say anywhere form 85-100% of the people that I arrested were willing to talk. They talked and told on their own family members. I had little respect for them.

I had on occasion to arrest this guy from Pineville and we took him to the Region III to question him. He seemed to cooperate but we still had to book him. He seemed awful friendly and kept looking out the window at a particular spot. As soon as he bonded out of jail he broke into our trailer at night and stole evidence on cases and other drugs that were at the trailer from being confiscated. We couldn't tell anyone this happened because we lost the evidence we had on certain cases. Within about three days of him doing this I had another informant that told me this guy had just left his house with a truckload of drugs. I pulled him over and I had a Metro narcotics agent with me. I told him to read him his right and place him under arrest. While I was searching the truck I heard a girl scream out what are you doing to this poor man. I looked up and my deputy, who was a very large man, had picked up the guy and threw him to the curb. I jumped out the truck and stopped him. The girl continued to scream and said she would call her dad who was a lawyer. We finally got to the Region with him and he was booked with burglary and possession. The screaming girl followed us to the Region. Shortly after arriving, the subject's attorney showed up. He used to be a judge and a good friend of mine. He kept saying he wanted to see his client and check him to see how bad we had beaten him up. Finally we allowed the attorney to talk to his client and we then booked him into jail. I never knew exactly what happened to this particular case. The deputy that was with me was so angry and I asked him why it wasn't his evidence locker. He said he was upset about the big pickle jar of pills that had come up missing. He was taking all the black molly pills to loose weight. He came across a bunch of these pills from arresting a pharmacist in Winnfield because he got scared of the trade on some black subjects who were coming from Alexandria to get their prescriptions filled. The black subjects threatened to burn his house. We pretended to be a pharmacist and we busted eight subjects that day. The pharmacist was scared and stated he was closing his store because he was tired of being threatened. He turned around and handed us a basket full of different kind of pills. He did close his store and went to work at a local pharmacy. In his condition he eventually was fired from his local job.

I was always being told not to work so much with the city and parish narcotics agents and that we should keep our investigations to ourselves. Personally I didn't see a need to do this because I got along well with everyone. One time an agent who was very incompetent I told him that I would use him and make over twenty distribution cases with him. This guy didn't know anything about police work and hated it. I took him and ran him with different informants and made over thirty distribution cases. After my boss and his bosses found out about it they wanted to turn it into a big publicity campaign. They wanted to have a big round up with the newspapers and the press. I reminded them they didn't want anything to do with the investigations and now they were interested. I rounded them up myself in about two day's time. As I had said earlier I wanted out of narcotics and they couldn't find a replacement for me. They suggested I stay around so I could be the next sergeant. This didn't set well with the agents sharing an office with me. Some of them were very ambitious. While going through the motions of being a dedicated agent all the corruption around me was bringing me down. One night I drove to my office and I knew so one was suppose to be there. We had already arrested one guy for burglary. When I saw the light on in my office I thought someone was burglarizing again. When I opened the door and walked into my office there sat the captain of the state police with a cardboard box in his hand. In the box was some evidence but most of its was marijuana that we didn't have any defendant for. In other words it was set to be destroyed. I asked him what was he doing with the box of marijuana and he said that he needed it for his wife and asked me if I was going to tell anyone. I told him "no, what's one more thing doing wrong." Just before that I had worked an undercover deal with a detective who was so messed up on drugs; I had to leave him asleep in the bed and covered up. He too later became captain of the police force. He was angry with me for leaving him in that state but I told him I knew he was safe and I couldn't bring him to his house in that condition. Right after this episode with the captain, my wife and I went to the first state police convention. Most troopers were a member of the union but I had never been to any conventions. My wife and my sergeant talked me into going. We were in a caravan of about fifteen state police cars and a few unmarked cars. They were driving well over the speed limit as we raced to the convention in Houma. Most of the officers were drunk and driving state police units. Several ran off the road. Some had to get another driver because they were too drunk to continue the drive. The convention was for the state policemen to get together and talk about different things and laws. It was to be a party and athletic competition and basically have a good time. I was puzzled as to how the state policemen were allowed to drive marked cars while under the influence. I entered into one competition and that being tennis. I had a few drinks before playing the game. I came in last and I could see my fate because several regional sergeants got together talking about me. They all were fighting on who was undercover first and how often.

I didn't think much of it at the time but I should have seen that my fate was determined. After playing tennis I walked back to my room and while doing so, I passed a door that smelled like marijuana was being used. I opened the door and there was the captain's wife and four state policemen smoking pot. This seemed to be very hypercritical so I left the room. I walked to a bar and I recognized someone I had been to college with. After talking to him for a short time he handed me some marijuana and said for me to leave so he could smoke his. This finished me off. I immediately went back to my hotel and my wife and I packed up and went back home. I couldn't see the difference in the policemen smoking pot or the guy at the bar who probably would have been arrested.

After the convention I worked around my home office for a short time mostly with parish narcotics. I tried to avoid getting called out undercover because I knew I was going to be called on a lot. I was wanted by many different agencies to work undercover and I was bunt out. I didn't want to be around drugs and I didn't feel any accomplishment in busting anyone. I saw policeman sleeping in their cars with prostitutes with their pants over the lights of the car to beating up suspects. I have to say that the worse law ever passed was allowing the local or any police agency to keep or seize in the name of narcotics money and properties of individuals, guilty or not.

This has led to the biggest part of police corruption. If a policeman finds any money at a house they seize it in the name of narcotics seizures. I have seen piggy banks taken that had money in it that belonged to children, furniture destroyed and various other items seized just to say they either bought it with narcotics money or hid narcotics in it before. Many times I had seen guns, furniture and other items seized during a search warrant at a policeman's house. After a gun was seized several of the officers would see who gets the gun first.

My last undercover investigation was in Lake Charles, LA. I previously described the investigation and prior to this investigation we were working on a Houston, Texas deal. We had just accomplished one that we lost because of the pill exchanging. I had another Houston deal going on and I left it with a narcotics agent to work on when I got through with Lake Charles investigation. I asked the agent to wait on the deal so we would have time to set it up properly. He kept on about going ahead with the deal and I told him no. He had developed while working in his office a sense that he was an inferior policeman and no one in his own office would trust him with any information. I told him to wait and I promised him he would receive the credit for this bust. He came down to Lake Charles and said he had to go ahead with the deal. I told him to wait because we didn't have everything cleared for us to go into another state. I got in touch with another agent and told him where I was going and that I would be right back.

The agent came to Lake Charles with two informants, which I knew very well the other informant helped me on previous busts. When they came to pick me up the other agent was pretty messed up. He had been taking black mollies and drinking beer. He said we needed to drive to the fifth ward in Houston, Texas to meet two black guys. This was an all black section in Houston that was known for violence. We had to stop the car several times so the other agent could take a leak and try to straighten up. We drove and met the two black subjects in fifth ward in Houston. After arriving and assessing the situation I felt that we should have had better back up. I didn't like it at all and I said so to the other agent. The other agent pulled out a wad of money and I didn't know how much it was. He said he was going to show them the money and let the subjects take him to the marijuana and get them to take it back to Alexandria. He said if we didn't go ahead with the deal we needed to buy some now to show our good faith. I told him no don't show the money. Immediately after the two black subjects arrived he pulled out the roll of money and showed it to them and said he was ready to make a deal. They wanted the informant to ride with them to go get the marijuana. He wouldn't give me the money so I told him to stay at the hotel and I got into the back seat of the car to go look at the marijuana. I told them that it wasn't that much money that the agent showed them and that I would ride with them to see the stuff. I told them they could bring the marijuana to Alexandria and then we would pay them. When they saw I didn't have the money they insisted the agent with the money go see the marijuana and not me. I took my partner to the side and I begged him not to do it. I told him that he or the money would not come back and we should just forget about it. The agent insisted he was going ahead and I should wait at the hotel. That was the last time I saw him alive. I waited in Houston until daybreak then I drove back to Lake Charles Troop D. I waited there until my sergeant called me and told me they had found my partner dead. I was to wait until they came to pick me up.

I stayed there until about noon worried to death thinking of what I should have done. I knew the deal was wrong but I did get clearance but not from your immediate sergeant. We waited in the parking lot and the informant smoked pot continuously because of his nervous condition. We had made a pact that if something went wrong the officer living would take the blame for anything. When my sergeant picked us up he drove us back to Harris County. I wasn't given any rights, all I remember is that I sat in a chair in a completely blacked out room except the light hanging over my head. I stayed in that position for two days. I was bombarded with question after question about why I was there. Every time I would try to dose off someone was right there to shake me to awaken me. After so long a time I became delirious and didn't know what to do. Finally I told them what they wanted to hear. I told them that we were down there to buy marijuana to bring back to Alexandria to sell. I couldn't take it any longer so I figured that's what they (The Texas Rangers) wanted to hear. Immediately after saying this they turned on the lights and escorted me to a room so I could sleep. I figured that I would be arrested but I wasn't. I came back to my office and was told not to do anything. After one day I was sent to Baton Rouge to take a battery of lie detector tests. I passed every one I was given which they didn't want to believe. I was told to return to my office by the lieutenant and was told everything seemed o.k. I was still not to do anything when I got back to my office because of it being election time for mayors and I had charges on both of their sons. It turned into a big political atmosphere that I couldn't control. I called the major and he promptly told my sergeant not to bother him any more. I could see the writing on the wall and then about four days passed and the lieutenant that handled internal affairs showed up at my office. He told me that I had to go with him to Monroe to take another polygraph test or if I refused I would be charged with a crime. I went with him to take another test, which I passed except it was very slanted. I wound up getting into an argument with the tester because I should have been told the questions that I had the answer and not some questions off the wall. He was truly there to try and catch me in a lie. I told the lieutenant to bring me back to my office and that this guy was a quack. When I got back to my office I was told to take two weeks off with pay, which meant I would probably be fired. After the two weeks off I had to drive to my office and turn my car in. plus my badge and identification. I was given a ride home I saw my baby daughter running across the yard and it suddenly dawned on me, I had nothing to drive and no money to spare. I think my sergeant cried more than I did when I was terminated. I think he knew they had done an injustice to me. He told me I needed to file an appeal to get my job back, which would have taken about a month. In this month's time I was offered many jobs by local police officers. One was in Pineville. I didn't want to fill out the application but I did and when the detective brought my application to the mayor he tore it up and through it in the trash. I had a lot of present narcotics agents that wanted me to help them by giving them my informants or being a snitch for them. I told them no. In this time period the state was contemplating hiring me back and putting me back through the police academy. We should call it re-institutionalizing me. In this much time I couldn't find a job but my wife found a job and I fished and sold the fish to make extra money. I saved all the money I could to hire an attorney. I was ready for my local appeal for my job back. In this time period I never heard from the state police of which I paid dues to. They never once tried to help me. I managed to buy a truck from a detective friend of mine for $100. I had to wire the doors for them to stay closed. In the daytime I would use this truck to pick up old roofing shingles that they would pay me to haul away. My daughter would always be with me because we couldn't afford a babysitter. I can remember one time being pulled over by a state policeman and when I got out the truck to show him my license he had been a friend of mine and when he saw me he immediately started crying to see me reduced to hauling shingles. I didn't fit the profile of a rich cop.

When my lawyer suggested I get a petition and get signatures saying they would back me, I didn't receive not one signature until I personally called the chiefs and commanders of different departments after a short conversation they all agreed to sign it and made everyone else sign it. I told them I was a respectable guy and I expected them to be.

I was fired from the state police either/or going to Houston without prior authorization or fooling around with people of disreputable character. This was what the police were basing their case on. I was going to discuss my case with my attorney as we traveled to Baton Rouge for my hearing. He was a former prosecutor with the Rapides Parish and had left there to be an attorney with the Camille Gavelle Firm. This was a highly noted firm and I thought I had the trust of this attorney, however, on the way to Baton Rouge he had to stop a lot of time and go to the rest room because he had contacted some form of venereal disease. Instead of talking about my case he wanted to know the symptoms of syphilis or what was know then as the claps. I felt like I was in a science class and I knew right then that I didn't have a chance. As for as authorization I told the only agent in the Lake Charles area where I was going because the supervisor was at a party at the Governor's Mansion in Baton Rouge. He got on the stand and told a lie. As far as fooling around with ill repute that is the only people I knew when I worked undercover narcotics.

As far as me testifying my lawyer seemed to have forgotten all we discussed on the trip down to Baton Rouge. He was too busy rubbing his crotch. I knew when we left the building that I had lost the case. All my attorney wanted to do was go home and be treated for his disease. At a later time I learned he was disbarred.

After returning home I felt the state police still wanted to hire me back through the academy. One agent that worked in my office wanted to make sergeant before I did. He had one of my old informants call me and he recorded the conversation so he could play it back to the internal affairs. I knew I was being recorded because of all the stopping and starting that the informant was doing on the phone. The first question he asked was if I wanted to bring marijuana back to this town so he could sell it for me. I knew then what was going on so I told him "yes, a truck load." He then asked me what was the best way to hide drugs. I told him to dig a big hole in the ground and put the marijuana in jars and dig them up as needed. I told him that was what I would do. The agent couldn't wait to play the tape to the internal affairs. This is when they said I must have really been a duty cop. Police getting fired was publicity enough but this created a ground swell because it was election time for mayors. One mayoral candidate used it for the best of his ability even as far as trying to get me arrested. I would throw things in the dumpster and he would have someone come behind me to retrieve what I had thrown away. Two city policemen detectives strictly assigned to watch and investigate me were my friends that I have worked with in the Metro section. The agent that was killed in Houston spent the night with one of them at their house. You can come to your own conclusion why he was so interested in investigating me. The other agent I had stopped him several times from planting evidence on different people.

It was hard for me to find work because every time I put in an application I would always hear two things, first was "why was I in Houston?" or the easiest one was I was over qualified because of my college. It was hard to hide from people that I had arrested or people that helped me. I had eventually got a job delivering mechanic clothing. I did this for about two weeks. On my last delivery I was on a four-lane highway and someone got out a car that I had previously arrested and wanted to fight. It was raining so I wanted to put the clothes up first. We rolled into a ditch while fighting. I loaded up after the fight and got in the truck with my muddy clothes and went to the clothing store and quit my job. The boss of the rental company wanted me to go to California to see why his son was killed and I told him no way.

I quit delivering clothes when I reached my top pay of $150/week. I really knew what an ex-con feels like when he goes to apply for a job. Finally after two weeks of quitting my job an informant I knew brought me a kilo of marijuana. He said you could probably help me get rid of this with all the people you know. I knew he didn't have the money to have this much marijuana so I was immediately suspicious. Not thirty minutes after he gave it to me there was a bayou behind my house and was full of rainwater. I immediately took the kilo unwrapped it and threw it into the bayou. The informant began yelling and trying to retrieve the marijuana. I was sitting on the bank watching it float away while police were pulling in my driveway. I immediately told them don't bother getting out your car. Drive to the end of the bayou and you can scoop it out before it hits the river. All I could remember was someone making a smart remark saying I thought I was being smart. I told him no I'm not crooked but don't push me.

I finally got another job. My old supervisor got me a job working at the A & P Supermarket. I was an Assistant Produce Manager. When I left some ten years later I was #1 Co-Manager in this larger store in Louisiana. The whole time I worked here I was constantly asked by detectives to be their informants or some sheriff's in other parishes wanted me to work for them as a contract agent.

I was told to look at my options and decide what I would do. I was even tried to be hired by two other supermarket chains to see who was stealing from their stores. I found that by helping any and all and by me being connected to prior informants I was always in the drug scene or criminal elements.

I was pretty broke financially so I thought I would help in Crime Stoppers that offered a $1,000 reward. I saw several of these cases but only collected one time. Most of them used excuses that they used other informants or didn't see why they should pay a crooked cop. Most of them were jealous.

The very first big thing I got into which I just happened to catch a shoplifter at A & P. He told me he would make it worth my while if I let him go instead of turning him in. The very next day they showed up at A & P with a truckload of guns. I didn't know whether to turn him in or not but yet I didn't know what to do with all the guns. I sold the guns from A & P where I kept them in the produce cooler. My boss allowed this when I gave him a gun to shut him up. After selling to anyone that was employed by the store I started getting a little scared. I sold more television sets than guns because they wouldn't keep long in the coolers. One guy I trusted on state police. I met with him and told him to check them out to see if they were hot. The police gave me $100 a piece for them. He immediately the next day said he had to see me in his office and I told him I was helping him with the guns and not going to jail. He wanted to know who I was getting the guns from. I told him I would drive him to the guy's house because he had television sets for me to pick up. I did not know but this was a ring going on from Shreveport. Two nights before my day off a detective from the sheriff's office asked me to come to A & P and asked me to help him on a few things. I didn't mind him so bad but I didn't trust him either. He told me there was a big burglary in Lecompte where a lot of jewelry had been stolen specifically watches. He said yes. I immediately rolled up both my sleeves and I had approximately eight watches on each arm. H was shocked and asked me if I was helping anyone else. I told him no and he begged me to help him solve the case. He never said anymore about the watches I had. I had sold the watches for $10 each. I told him I wanted $160 from him. I told the deputy another man was due back with more watches and chains. Sure enough the guy showed up with the merchandise and was arrested. He asked me what I wanted out of it and I told him nothing. He was angry at this comment because I wasn't going to help him.

After turning in the gun deal all my supervisors at work had gotten in trouble. He wanted to arrest them but I told him no that I would buy all the guns back and turn them over to him.

From the time I was fired until several months leading up to my appeals, everyone came to me for help. One tried to get me on with his department but the Mayor tore up the application. Although I was working full time at A & P it seemed like I had never left under cover narcotics. I was still seeing crooks and good guys. This went on for about a year but everyone was stealing so much out of the grocery store and I couldn't resist. Managers, full time employees, everyone was stealing and I went along with it until I made Assistant Manager at the store. This time I thought since I was the Assistant Manager I would fire them for stealing but I couldn't. My full time grocery stockers and myself really started stealing. A whole freezer of rib eye steaks was stolen in one night. We stole two trucks full of beer. I drove the beer to my uncle's place and sold them to him for his strip bar. It seemed like that I was on a mission with the sole purpose of making more money. I had a close family member who had connections and he started bringing in pounds of marijuana. I was selling over one hundred pounds a week and barely getting my money back. I was fronting a lot of the money with intentions of getting my money back and a lot of people never paid up. I was getting tired of it because I wasn't making any money and a police friend of mine asked me to stop selling. I would still sell them marijuana for their parties and go in buildings that they were patrolling and steal the contents. The police that were supposedly guarding wound up with just about anything that was in storage.

I told him I had to stop. I always had this thing in my head when they would probably wind up selling me out. Then one night the man that was about to be sheriff of our parish asked me if I wanted to be in charge of his narcotics department. I really respected this man but I was so messed up that I told him I would have to think about it. He said he wouldn't ask again. If I was interested to come see him. As soon as detectives and narcotics heard about it they were determined to get me. They did not want me to have this position because they thought I was crooked. About a week after this I drove to Ball, LA to pick up one of my employees. When I got there I recognized a car that was on crime stoppers and it was in his driveway. The man they were looking for that drove this car was an escapee from Rapides Parish jail and had a $1000 reward on his head.

I knew I would surely get the $1000. I found out where the guy was staying. I gave this information to a detective I knew, not knowing that he was one that hated me most. I waited the weekend and I heard the guy had been arrested. I called the detective for my reward money. The detective and his partner met me on a secluded road and pulled a gun on me and said they didn't use my information so they could keep the money for themselves. I told them I would look into this and if he needed the money that bad he could stick it up his ass.

About two days after this episode I went to the courthouse to turn in some NSF checks. The District Attorney's office is on the same floor as the Sheriff's office. I tried to avoid everyone. The detective saw me and came up to me. He pulled his gun, cocked it and put it to my temple. He said he would kill me if I were going to the District Attorney's office to turn him in over the $1000 reward. I fell to my knees and told him not to get crazy I was just bringing in NSF checks. He put the gun back in his holster and said that the next time he sees me he will pull it and use it. The detectives would not settle for this. They were out to ruin me one way or another. The next day his detective friend ran a search warrant on my house for a large quantity of drugs. He came to my house with about twelve cars representing the state police, Rapides Parish Sheriff's office, detectives and narcotics agents. There were some officers from Camp Beauregard. He tried to do the best he could on the search warrant but I was informed ahead of time from a former state policeman that they were on their way to my house. I had about one hundred pounds of marijuana here and I kept it in the chicken house. The officers didn't make an attempt to go back there. They destroyed my house as best they could. I had a brief case that had some search warrants that I kept when I was employed by the state police. I also had an ounce of marijuana in an evidence envelope that I had retrieved while a state policeman. I also had five uniforms. The state policeman that sound the envelope of marijuana put it in his pocket and told me not to worry he would get rid of it for me.

I had a cocker spaniel dog that was in heat and the drug dog was a male and he couldn't do his job. They asked me to put my dog in the storage room because their drug dog was being distracted. While I was putting the dog away I had about two ounces of loose marijuana in a bag and I put the marijuana in my pocket and let the plastic bag blow in the wind. The detective handed me the affidavit of the search warrant and I told him that he had the wrong address and the wrong color of my house now what are going to do. He walked around outside and I went in to use the restroom. I took the marijuana from my pocket and flushed it. When the detective heard the toilet flush he asked me what I was doing. I told him I was using the toilet. He told me I needed to follow him. He said sit here I need to go back and change the address on the search warrant. I told him if he leaves he needed to take all the rest of his guys with him and when he did leave he lost his probable cause to search. He then asked me what should do. You might offer me a permission to search slip. They were already searching. He handed me the slip to sign and I signed someone else's name to it. He was very mad at me.

He said I could make this search warrant work. They searched the whole house and found nothing.

The dog kept smelling my hot water heater but nothing was in there. It was very cold outside he looked at me and asked me why was I shaking; I only had a tee shirt on. I told him I told him I was scared he would frame me. I told him I wanted to walk everywhere he went. I watched him the whole time he was in my house. They confiscated a scale; ice chest and a dollhouse play school scale. As they were leaving the evidence taken spilled everything under my carport. I immediately told him oops there goes your chain of evidence. They then walked to their cars and he got in his car and closed the door. I told him then he should have called me and next time I would have coffee and hot chocolate for them. I then said once you get in your car and leave your search is over and your probable cause has ended. I told him you and I both know this search warrant wasn't any good. That he had done the search for political reasons. He immediately got out his car and made everyone come back to search my house over again.

One other thing I kept at my house that should be mentioned was about four hundred rolled ounces of marijuana in a trash can on my carport and I had forgotten it was there. I would make an annual trip to Flatwoods, LA and buy all the home grown that the loggers in Flatwoods would grow. The money from the marijuana sale went to buy Christmas presents. I didn't make much money on this all of the marijuana needed to be shipped to Arkansas to a man who was a state official. He could have been a policeman for all I knew. This I did for two years and I would be lucky if I made five dollars on every ounce. I thought I was making our pretty good.

They were really using me for what I got out of it for holding the marijuana. I think the marijuana came from Orange, Texas but I never asked any questions.

When I went to Flatwoods to pick up the marijuana, logger trucks would line up twenty deep to come see me. This was all set up by a prominent councilman in the area to help the locals. This was a bad deal because homegrown marijuana didn't sell good but I stuck to my word and they couldn't wait for me to show up.

I felt the search warrant was done totally to discredit me in the eyes of the sheriff and so they wouldn't have to hire me. Several deputies that searched my house told him the search warrant wasn't any good. While he was searching I answered my phone and his partner was on the other line so I told him what was going on. He was upset because he wasn't told anything about it. I told him "Oh you wanted to come too" and he said, "No, there is no reason to come." After the search warrant it got around that I was a crook and the sheriff never offered me a job again.

As I stated earlier I had four complete state police uniforms and blank search warrants. I used these uniforms and search warrants to run my own task force. I would dress up at least three of my stock boys in uniform and then I would type a search warrant and have a black stock clerk to sign the warrant because he had a nice handwriting like a judge. We ran about ten search warrants with no problems. No one had a gun on our searches. Just the uniform would scare the people. Most of the search warrants we went on were Air Force employees and this was during the time England Air Force was still active. We would use the sneak and peak methods to see if they had any drugs which are still used today. This method was illegal then as it is today. I firmly believe if you can't get proper probable cause no search warrant should ever be run on anyone's house. However in this day and time they believe that the bill of rights don't mean anything. Until this country goes back to the way it was suppose to be people's rights will constantly be abused. I never made up any information on anyone or deemed them to be a person of interest.

As I was stating earlier I ran at least ten search warrants and we used plexicuffs. If anyone ran out the house we just let them go we didn't chase them. We would allow them to think they go away. We would confiscate up to thirty pounds of marijuana sometimes. I was the only one with a badge and on the last search warrant, which was on Kent Street the real police showed up. He asked me if we needed any help or did he need to call in the Metro narcotics to help us. I told him we had it under control. I had everyone handcuffed and I gave him $20 for his concern so he could buy himself supper. I knew this would be the last warrant as it was too close and our luck was about to run out. We left six people handcuffed and lying face first on the floor and I told the people that we had handcuffed just to be still and that a paddy wagon was on the way so all of them could fit. These guys were enlisted in the Air Force so how were they going to report that someone took their marijuana. WE put a pillow under each one's head so it would be a little comfortable. They thanked us for being so kind and not reporting to their commander. We got about eight pounds of marijuana out this house. We got in two cars and drove off my stockers removed the uniforms so I could have them laundered. I told them to sell the marijuana fast and we would split the money. I had a lot of opportunities to do this more often.

We did this quite a few times until I decided it was time to quit and they then searched my house and took all the uniforms and my blank search warrants. I did not have a proper judge to sign the warrants and he was a black subject that lived on the bayou along with eight other brothers and sisters. I got to say one thing my guys looked good in their uniforms even spit shined their shoes. Another ting that bothered me was the real narcotics agents wasn't running many search warrants but I knew that all we took from the people and that they wouldn't turn us in for taking their drugs. Air Force people were the easiest ones to fool and I would say that we did this over a three-week period and we stayed busy.

After the search warrant and various other things that were said about me I couldn't figure out if I was a policeman or a snitch or who was really a policeman. Every time I went anywhere there were detectives pulling me over and asking for my help or either what was I up to. I got to the point where I would beg them to leave me alone and I wanted out of this shit and tired of helping them with their jobs and them getting credit for it. I remember telling some of the policemen that they couldn't detect their own ass. They seemed that I knew about any kind of drugs coming into this town. I felt like I needed to straighten up and stay at my job. However out of the blue as I was getting off work and walking into the parking lot a detective that is presently a sheriff and his partner arrested me in the parking lot of A & P for armed robbery of a bank. They took me to the interrogating room at the Rapides Sheriff's office and started questioning me and I looked at the future sheriff and I said do you actually believe that I can actually do something like that. It seemed to bother him that he brought me in for questioning knowing what kind of policeman I was. He then brought me back to work. He told me I keep getting a bad rap from everyone. I said I was trying and it seemed like everyday something was happening. I had white powder on my clothes when I was picked up which was from fighting with someone I had arrested while a policeman. We were fighting in the store down the flour isle and we had scattered flour everywhere. I did beat the guy up pretty bad. He thought he was going to get even with me finally. I had some stock boys and myself push him out the door. My reputation as a crook grew as they ran the search warrant on my house and all the other problems I was having. They had picked me up for armed robbery because they found a pistol that was registered to me but stolen and it was used in an armed robbery then thrown in the ditch in front of my house. I had sold the pistol to a friend of mine while working as a state police and his son used it in the robbery.

It was no surprise to me that one night as I was leaving the store a former policeman came up to me and said he needed to talk to me. He took me to a hotel in Alexandria where five or six other police were waiting in the room. After getting to the room they started laying out a plan where by myself and a brother to one of the guys would use a big truck and chain and pull out the deposit boxes out of the night drops of the area banks.

The catch was that these police that were in the room would be working in that section of the city when we pulled out the alarm. It would also be on the night I would make a large deposit from the store so we were sure to have a large amount of money. They told me the complete plan and asked me if I was ready to do it. I asked them why they thought I would do something like this. I told them since they were all city policeman what would happen if a deputy were to respond while we were still there. They said if that were to happen they would take care of it, which could have meant they would go so far as to shoot him. I said you can count me out. I don't want any part of this. Two of the police in the room got extremely mad. They said we couldn't let him leave the room now because he knows all us and the plan. The police that took me to the room told him that I wouldn't say anything and they should allow me to leave and return to my job. They said we should shoot him and that way we wouldn't have to worry about him. I told one of them that you all are big about threatening people but I don't want anything to do with this shit. I said I don't want to know when or how or anything else you do. After I got dropped off at the store I felt really bad from becoming what I thought was a well-respected policeman to be thought of as a crook of this severity.

After we had a meeting at the hotel about three days later I went to make a deposit and there was my dad's construction company working on the night deposit box. It seemed that someone had pulled the box from the wall with a big truck. This happened to two or three banks in the area. There were quite a few policemen involved in this even the chief of city police who was retired. He was in charge of the investigation and he just couldn't seem to solve the case. I feel as if a few state policemen were in on this. I vaguely mentioned this to the chief and he seemed nervous and scared and transferred to the northern part of the United States.

A few months later I met up with a vendor as I checked him at the door. He was talking to me about cocaine and asked if I wanted to buy or sell some. I told him I didn't want any but I might be able to sell some for you because I know of some local attorney's that would be interested. He said he could get his cousin in Miami who worked in a jewelry store and could bring a large quantity down if he thought I could get rid of it. About a week later he got his friend in town and I met with him at the Colonial Apartments. I set it up with a state police friend of mine to go make a control buy so they could run a search warrant on the room. They gave me the money to buy some of the cocaine. I bought a small amount but saw a lot more. I told him not to call anyone else I would have my lawyer friends and they would probably buy the rest of the supply. I left there and the state police immediately pulled me over to get the small amount of cocaine that I had bought. He said I don't know if I should go in right now this quickly might burn you. I told him I didn't care they had better hurry or it will be gone. They ran a search warrant and they arrested the subject and got a large amount of cocaine. This is the first time I got paid $1000 from crime stoppers. I was running the 4-H fair in poultry and he came and paid me. This sounds good helping the state police for the $1000 but all it did was antagonize the Metro narcotics, which consisted of the parish officers. They wanted me to help them and they thought they owned me. The sergeant of this officer was mad because we had a meeting before the search warrant and he assured me that they didn't do things like they use to when I worked there. This made me mad so I told him "what? Ya'll don't work undercover for a month and fuck and woman you can but you can't make cases like you used to." I told him there wouldn't be any problems and no guns. I wish they would have gotten the third guy but as he pulled up to the hotel he saw the cops searching and he pulled away and picked his wife up and immediately moved back to his hometown of Oakdale. This is where he later became an Oakdale City Policeman. He still owes me money today for a hot gun, marijuana and for a phone bill I had to pay for him. He would get the marijuana and sell to two or three Coca Cola truck drivers. As you see I didn't make much money in selling marijuana because people were constantly shorting me or not paying me at all. I knew I had to get out of it because all I was doing was loosing money. The only way to sell marijuana and make any profit is to find a better connection for a cheaper price. The idea of making money is to undercut your competition like a Wal-Mart store. I went into other ventures while being employed at A & P for some ten years. In driving down the road you might notice vendors stands along the road selling produce. At night when they needed to put their produce up to keep it cool I would rent one of two coolers to about six vendors for $25 a week. The produce manager caught me. I convinced him that I couldn't run them out yet because they had paid for the month. I split the money with the manager to let them finish out the month. One day we made a bet in the store that our licensed florist could hold a pallet on her stomach while laying on the floor with 1000 pounds of potatoes on top the pallet. I bet everyone $5 that she could and she did it and we split the money with her. She probably didn't feel too much of anything because she was messed up on marijuana and Xanax.

While in produce I witnessed wholesale stealing of meat from the meat market. I raised a bunch of chickens at my house so I carried a box of loose lettuce leaves to them everyday. Under the lettuce leaves was a rack of rib eye steaks. We saw the meat market manager take loads of turkeys when it was Thanksgiving season but no one wanted to turn him in because they were all guilty of doing the same thing. I later transferred to Dairy Manager and the store manager would get drunk and make a double order of milk without me knowing. All milk is dated so I had to get rid of the excess. I would have to help him out the store everyday because he was drunk. He had caught his wife and babysitter together. I would have one of my stock boys to drive him home very day. To get rid of the excess milk I would load up my truck from the back of the store and pull down to some of the pour sections of town in Alexandria and sell it for 50 cents a gallon.

Another big financial tragedy was when they put new freezers in the store. They ordered supplies for the freezers and after the food was stocked the freezers were stuck in defrost mode. I had to pull my truck behind the store again and fill my truck with the frozen goods. Most of this had to be thrown away. One bad thing happened when we tried to sell the food the neighbor's dog ate so much Saulsberry steak that he rolled over on his back and suffocated.

I had a sixty-foot driveway and it was line up on both sides with frozen food dinners. I fed all the neighborhood animals and anything that was good I gave away. My neighbor was sick about loosing his dog to saulsberry steak dinners. I couldn't make much money on this deal so the dinners that were still good we would drive down sections of disadvantaged people and throw the dinners in their yards much like the army did when they dropped food from planes in the military. When I left the dairy department I was transferred to number one Assistant Manager. This is when I tried to stop the stealing and I was approached about doing the bank jobs and I was in charge of doing the large bank deposits every day. There were a few deposits that came up missing with cash and checks but I never took any of the money. We had one manager that was in charge of the cashiers. She was the only on that failed the polygraph about the deposits. Another occasion the cashier's manager accidentally put the deposit bag in someone's grocery bag. Finally the store got two more managers for stocking. One had to work nights because he would never take a bath. The other could only workdays because if he worked nights he would get drunk and his stockers would party all night. I had to pull several twenty-four hour shifts to keep things going. Then what made things worse of all we had a regional director from New Orleans who thought he was God. He would come into the store and try to find as many things wrong as he could and threaten people the whole time. He sexually harassed just about every female employee in the store. He would beg me to get them to go out with him. All the girls were frightened of him so I had to escort the girls to their car as he was waiting in the parking lot for them. I had to threaten to whip his ass many times and he in turn would threaten to fire me. One time I saw him in the car with a black girl that worked at the store and she said you don't have to worry about him he couldn't get a hard on. He didn't return to the store after that because he was being referred as "little dick". With the deposits missing and bad inventories the manager was going to be fired and when they bring in a new manager a new broom always sweeps clean. I was transferred to another store as Assistant Manager came to the other store I was at to fuss at me. As he was fussing at me I turned my back to him and starred at a small hole in a brick wall. He said what are you doing turning your back to me I said you see this hole in the wall, I have more respect for this hole in the wall than you. I was transferred back to the big store and demoted to a stocker with one helper. I was given impossible tasks to do, which they knew I couldn't do so I knew they wanted to fire me. However, while we were unloading the truck from a lift that I told them it needed to be fixed. The hydraulics on one side of the lift would give out. As we were lowering a heavy pallet of can goods it gave way. I pushed the guy out the way so it wouldn't crush him so it fell on me and crushed one of my vertebrae. I had to go out on workman's compensation and this they could not stand. With them watching my house and the police bothering me it became too much. One night I was having a barbeque at my house and I purposely invited the new store manager. As the police were watching from their shiny new car they saw I was in a large brace up to my neck. I walked to the end of my driveway and asked them to leave me alone. They said don't look like you are two hurt you can be outside having a barbeque. I then pulled out a pistol and shot two holes in their new car. I told "little dick" I would have him arrested for sexual harassment. I had another job line up before leaving A & P. I worked for private detectives. I was hired by a competitive store chain to work undercover in his store to catch his employees stealing.

Another job I held while at A & P I took a week off and told my wife that I was going to help re-do a store in Baton Rouge. A new A & P was about to be opened. However, I was called by a friend of mine from California that said he was working for the CIA, which I could prove or disapprove. He said he had a way that I could make $5,000 cash with a job down in Mexico. I asked him what I needed to do and he said he would tell me when he arrived. I was not to discuss this with anyone else. We went across the border in a new four-wheel drive truck. We had calling cards with different Mexican names on it. We also had guns, which looked like they belonged to the military. We drove to different marijuana fields and set them on fire in the name of eradication and we would leave calling cards of the other growers. This worked for about three days and we had to haul ass out of there as soon as possible. They caught onto this pretty fast. I remember destroying weapons and getting the truck across the border. We left the truck in a lot in El Paso. I was given $2,500 up front and promised $2,500 after the fact but I never received the last half. I drove home and swore to myself I would never do this again.

I quit A & P and went back to school to become a schoolteacher. I didn't quite finish and I was offered a job at the United States Post Office.

I was lacking maybe one semester before I would be able to receive my teaching certificate. I really didn't know if I wanted to work at the post office until the personnel told me the salary I would be making. I delayed starting at the post office to receive my teaching degree. I was only thirty-four years old when I started the post office. I really didn't want to go back to any situations but I figured the people at the post office would be more professional and a better valued class of people. I figured here I wouldn't have to worry about being around drug deals or working any police functions. Well, after the first month of working at the post office my supervisor met me in the restroom and due to my age, which they had an age cut off, offered me to be a postal inspector. I asked him was it like being a policeman in the post office. He said first of all I would have to go to Baltimore, Maryland for training and then work undercover at some post office to check out employees. He told me they needed someone bad on the docks was all black and about one hundred of them with no white employees. He said he had just looked at my qualifications and said I would be perfect for the job. I told him I didn't want to do undercover police work. I told him people already didn't like me for the other policeman telling tales and lies about me.

After working at the post office about six months, no one in their life is perfect but this is one of the most corrupt places I have ever worked. I heard of kickbacks from machines that didn't work sorting the mail. I saw big bosses come down to Alexandria to supposedly to inspect us but they were coming to meet their girlfriends. A complete list of violations there were alcoholics, drug abuse, hiring relatives, sex, and stealing mail and money orders so they could buy crack cocaine and break in the vaults to steal stamps. The short overview of the post office was they could make money with less supervision and less employees. They are on the same level as most private companies as when a full time employee retires or quits they replace them with a part time employee with no benefits.

This is a government agency that's just as guilty as other large agencies not wanting to provide benefits. It is a good salaried job but a lot of employees are veterans and mostly from Vietnam and they all had problems they developed while in the armed services. Equipment doesn't mean anything to them they would just as soon leave something in the rain and go buy more. As I said earlier after working there for a while the morale was low. There were a lot of tension between supervisors and employees. The union that everyone was a member of only collected money and didn't bother helping where they were needed. Instead of jobs being accessed by full time employees they were interested in filing a grievance for someone who thought they lost thirty minutes in overtime pay.

The post office turned out to be a big circus. Supervisors would always say the mail got out whether it did or didn't so they could get their bonus checks. These checks meant everything to a supervisor especially the top ones. This was sort of like telling a policeman we would do a search warrant and keep all the money we could find. There were no performance standards and some people were actually scared to discipline because past service problems from the Vietnam War. Several people had the keys to the supply room and that's where things were always stolen. This post office was not considered that big. Can you imagine what would be delivered to the larger post offices? They were always updating mail sorter machines to be more efficient which caused more errors with the mail. The actual hand sorting was gradually being replaced by automation. The hand sorting of the mail, I would say, was ninety-nine percent correct but too slow for the post office standards. Mail began dealt with in volume by feet and weight instead of accuracy. The delivery people were suppose to deliver so much mail in so much time which is still happening today. I know of an instance where a postal worker was made postal worker of the year but only a short time later instead of carrying mail he was also selling crack cocaine from his mail truck. Most of the people from the post office were looking for drugs or had access to some. This is due in part on restricted sick leave, which is the first step to being suspended. It could be seen that a person with the proper contacts could make a lot of money on postal workers. On a legally basis I know collectively employees would buy at least $500. in pills. I haven't been to the post office in a while as I permanently injured my knee.

While working at the post office I took advantage of some of the people who wanted to buy pills. Most of these people do not work at the post office any longer. By taking advantage I would help them find what they were looking for. This led me back into the police again. One weekend I learned that a prominent black member was going to set up my self and a friend of mine. Prior to working a deal with him I had to sign an amnesty release saying that I would help them and not break the law any more. In other words this gave me the immunity of all the past crimes that I might have done. I agreed to help this one agent but I couldn't find him. On a Sunday and this guy I knew kept calling me telling me that he had dour pounds of marijuana that he had stolen and he would sell it to me cheap but I had to hurry and get it. I knew this guy as a former informant of mine and he had set up a friend of mine to go to jail and I didn't trust him. It took me after looking at the marijuana about an hour for someone to meet me and then go and act like he was interested in purchasing it. Finally they sent an agent that was brand new at this. This would be his first case. Apparently they must have told a lot of lies about me because he was scared to death. I told him the whole deal and assured him nothing bad would happen. He said if it did he had a pistol and he would use it on me first. We rode over and met the guy. He didn't have anyone with him. Immediately after pulling up the guy with the marijuana started hollering that the guy that had brought me to the scene was a cop. I told him to shut up and that I wouldn't bring a police with me to do anything. I asked him where the marijuana was and he pointed to the bushes. He started walking towards the marijuana and asked the policeman to follow him and I would stay at the truck. The police officer had just stared in narcotics. He was somewhat scared and I told him to go ahead that he didn't have anything to worry about. As he was following behind the suspect he pulled his pistol and I yelled at him to put the gun away and let the suspect get the tub of marijuana from the buses and not himself. After they go back to the truck the suspect put it in the truck and asked for his money. I told him to get the stuff from the truck and pay the suspect for the marijuana. He said to me that he didn't have enough money on him to buy it. I told the suspect that I would give him the money. He handed the tub of marijuana to the officer. Instead of the officer taking the evidence he put the bucket back in the truck and flashed his police badge I said to him "Tell the suspect what he is arrested for" The policeman looked at me and asked me what to say. I told the police to show his badge and tell him he was under arrest. He asked me what for. Sharply I replied, "Tell him he is under arrest for distribution of marijuana". I then told him to handcuff the suspect. The suspect asked me why was I doing this to him and I said this is payback now turn around and get against the truck so I can handcuff you. The police was searching the truck and I told him to stop and come read the suspect his rights. The police asked me how do I do this. I had to tell the officer what to say which he finally did. He then said the forgot to bring his portable to call the office for the suspect to be hauled away. I told him he could use my phone but I expected him to pay me back for the phone bill. I wasn't trying to degrade the new policeman but to show this was his first bust. He said to me that he was worried when he was assisted by me. He had heard a lot of bad stuff on me and I told him he couldn't believe all the stories he had heard. He gave me his phone number and asked if I would help him again. I told him I didn't know. I heard from him the very next night.

He wanted me to meet him behind a store in Pineville to talk to me. The person I was previously helping was angry with me when he found out I was helping the new officer. I met him behind the store and it seemed as if he became more positive about himself and he wanted me to immediately tell him if I was going to work with him or not. He wanted me to sign a confidential paper stating I would work with him. I told him I didn't think I needed to sign anything but after that a whole stack of savings bonds, belonging to some in Alexandria went missing. A black person had stolen them form her then sold them to me. He told me he didn't handle this sort of thing but he would radio someone to tend to the matter of the savings bonds. He radioed someone and his exact words were "one of my boys has stolen savings bonds and I don't handle things like this." After talking on the radio he handed the bonds back to me and said hang on to them until the other officer comes. I looked at him and said "I am not anyone's boy" I got out the car and told him I didn't want anything to do with him. He asked me was I going to help him or he would bust me. He then threw a beer bottle at me and missed. The very next day he called me on my cell phone while I was making hospital runs and asked me what was I doing. I said to him "you don't know?". He said no and I replied if you don't know you don't need to know. He then asked again if I would help and again I said no I will not help you. He was angry and told me he would bust my ass. I sad I've got to go you are running up by bill and you haven't paid me from previous use.

It seemed to be hard to get away from police work and find some other type work that didn't involve police work. I came across an Arab man who owned a convenience store. After talking to him for a couple weeks he was unlike the rest of the people I had met. I met a lot of these Arab people by selling chickens and ducks. I had a cousin to marry an Arab. One thing about this group of people that they have no respect for the law or pay taxes and was under the belief that if they got in trouble they could always go back to their country. After dealing with this guy, and he was wealthy, I started meeting other Arabs. He and three more Arabs stick out in my memory. My son and I were feeding the chickens and ducks when about three of the Arab men drove into my driveway. They were well dressed. I had about twenty-five chickens in a cage on the ground and he said he wanted to buy all of them. I knew he had the money as he was drive a BMW vehicle. I told him that I didn't feel up to chasing chickens but I had bags to put them in if I could get my son to chase them. He told me no problem, we won't have to chase any of them he left and came back from his vehicle and went to the back of my yard. He had a machine gun. My son was scared and I asked him why he needed that gun. He asked where the chickens were. I pointed to the chickens in the pen and he put a clip in the machine gun and racked the gun across the ground several times killing all the chickens. I told my son to pick up the dead chickens and put five per bag and place them in the trunk of his car neatly and not to mess the car up. He started laughing along with the guys that were with him. One of the Arab men said "He doesn't fool around does he?" He paid me top dollar for the chickens and said he would come back later. I told him not to come back too soon. I me another Arab and he also had a convenience store. He was big into buying guns. It didn't matter whose or where they were. He told me he was shipping them to New York where they would be shipped elsewhere. This one Arab, that was wealthy, opened a brief case while in his store to display $100,000. He said he carried this amount with him always. He asked me if I could get him kilos of cocaine.

I probably couldn't but I quoted him $20,000. per kilo. I told him I would get back with him tomorrow. I called a friend of mine that I had previously helped and I have him the run down. The next day I went to meet the Arab man that wanted the kilos and I was wired so the police could hear the conversation. I told him that I could get him five kilos of cocaine and he told me he would give me $20,000. per kilo and pay me an extra $10,000 if I would bring the cocaine to him in Rapides Parish. He would also give me another $10,000. If I would drive the cocaine to his relatives in New York. He said his relatives would give him $40,000 per kilo and he would pay me my $10,000 first. This is all discussed on tape. The Arab man told me that his relatives in New York would transfer the cocaine to an Arab country in return they would ship the equivalent value of heroine back to New York. I told him I would be ready in one week. I left his place and went to the command center van where they were taping the recordings. They told me they didn't know if they could handle something this big. I told them I knew who I had to talk to and I left. I tried to avoid this Arab man as much as possible until the subject never was discussed again. The deal blew over like the wind. Nothing was given or received.

For some reason it seemed that selling animals you met people that dealt with drugs. I was raising and hatching ducks. Everyone in town pretty much knew I had birds. A friend of mine went fishing with a guy and he and his wife had just split up. His wife was living back with her mother in Ball, Louisiana and the story he told them was the local narcotics agents pulled over a produce truck and in the truck they confiscated fifteen kilos of cocaine. He told my friend they were keeping the drugs at his wife's mother's house. For some reason, after finding this out, about two weeks later the mother-in-law called me and wanted to buy some ducks from me.

She wanted a pair of Mallards. I told her I would bring them over but she said she wanted to come get them. I insisted that I would bring them to her because I wouldn't be home. I got to her house and went into her back yard. She grabbed the ducks from me to clip the wings. I told her that we could handle it. I cut the wings and then looked toward her shed. I walked toward her shed and pretended to be interested in the lawn mower. She told me that the lawn mower was broken and I make up a story that I saw a rat run across. She said she thought the shed was locked. At that instant my son had turned the knob and the door opened exposing to myself and my son fifteen bricks wrapped in plastic and on top the bricks was a metal box with red letters reading RPSO. My son looked at me and asked what it was. I told him and we immediately left. I told the lady good bye and I left her side gate unlocked on purpose. I had planned to return at dark and take the cocaine. I was going to give it to the sheriff himself. When I returned that night to her house I could only make a turn around on her road because there were three unmarked narcotic cars there. I don't know how many were involved but they were having certain people selling the cocaine for them. About one week after I left her house she phoned me and cursed me out. She knew then why I had came over there and she wanted to know who had told me about the cocaine. I told her I didn't know what she was talking about and she then hung up on me. About one week after that my friend and I were pulled over and told that if we said anything at all they would kill us.

Houston

I was once a state police officer for the state of Louisiana for four years. I was fired from my position, which was at the time a narcotics investigator. The reason they fired me was because I associated myself with people of irrepute. I thought this was ironic having worked narcotics for the Louisiana State Police. I was fired in 1977 and from that time until presently I have been harassed by just about every police agency in my area and others that I probably don't know of. I was accused of being involved with being a part of just about any crime, however, at he same time these same agencies consistently asked me to find out crimes from murders to arranging narcotics deals. I can say that I have helped on a few things only to get the crime stoppers reward in which I never collected on. They always found a reason not to pay me because they thought I always knew where the drugs were or had something behind it. Besides being harassed by police, I was constantly having to fight people who I busted when I was a state policeman.

I had made a few chartered bus trips to Mexico back in the early 1990's. At that time I had met a customs agent that works on Mexico and the United States border. We became friends because I assisted him in setting up a Mexican with one hundred boxes of 90 count of the date rape drug. He gave me his card and asked me any time I came down to that area or wanted to help him just let him know. Back in August of 2000 I had met a friend of mine who was attending college in Monroe at Louisiana Tech. He started talking about the drug ecstasy and told me he could get me some. He had told me he would be going to Mardi Gras in New Orleans and would call the following Monday and introduce me to a friend he knew that went to Louisiana Tech. who previously lived in Boston. This friend from Boston would hollow out large candles and fill them with ecstasy pills then seal it back. He was shipping approximately 70 pills per candle and was sending this all over the United States. I told my friend that I would like to meet this guy. I didn't expect to hear back until the Monday after Mardi Gras.

I called the customs agent and told him what I had and I knew that they had the potential to help me on this. He put me in contact with the DEA agent from New Orleans that he knew wasn't crooked. I spoke to the agent briefly and he told me to watch my back and he would travel to meet me to take over.

Instead of waiting till Monday like originally planned, my friend called me Friday before and he stated that he had to see me in the Wal-Mart parking lot at 7:30. I told him there was no way to meet at Wal-Mart he then suggested Ryan's Steak House. I told him I would try to be there. I got to Ryan's parking lot at approximately 8:00 p.m. and he was waiting which should have told me something. When se saw me pull up he immediately jumped in my truck on the passenger side. He said that the other guy would definitely meet me on Monday and he wanted to probably trade cocaine for ecstasy. He was taking about trading kilos for large amounts of ecstasy. This guy told me the guy had a lot of influence with the professional Wrestling Associate from Boston. I then asked if I had to go to Boston or meet with them here locally. He told me I would be able to make some deals here but in the end I would have to travel to Boston. H then pulled out cocaine from his pocket and said they wanted this quality. I told him o.k. I knew what they wanted it had to be hard and rocky. No sooner did I say this a truck with hunting lights pulled up to my truck. I asked him what was going on. I could tell he wasn't too nervous. I told him not to remove anything from his pockets and put your hands on the dash. I told him if you take your hands off the dash I would knock the hell out of him. By this time someone dressed in camouflage ran up to my truck pointing a pistol at me and ordered me out the truck. He told me he was a narcotics agent. He told me to keep my hands up. He asked me what we were doing there. I said, "we are talking and I am going to get my wife something to eat at Ryan's." I asked him what the problem was. He told me "you have a drug deal going on don't you." I said, "no." I said "officers what do you want me to do hold my hands up or open the door. I can't open the door with my hands up." I told him I didn't have a weapon and if I can put my hands down I will unlock the door and get out. When I put my hands down I slipped my shoe down ad put $600 inside my sock. I left $300 in my front pocket. I got out the truck and he patted me down. He didn't find anything but the $300 and he took it. They searched the other guy and found 13 grams of cocaine and

Gary L. Bordelon

money. They took the cocaine and his money and laid it out on my truck bumper and took pictures. They handcuffed him but not me. I waited about thirty minutes through this ordeal and they brought in a drug-sniffing dog. They ran through my truck about twenty times and never found anything. The dog never alerted to anything in the truck and he never barked at the cocaine laid out on my bumper. The dog finally broke loose from the handler and ran to the guy's car and began scratching up the door. At this time I was standing by some of the agents that arrived on the scene. I had a hand on each officer's shoulder and I said "looks like the dog wants in that car as I pointed to the guys care." I told them I didn't know whom the car belonged to. They would keep dragging the dog back to my truck and he would run around the truck more but still found nothing. The dog looked as if he would urinate on my seat. I told them if he urinated on my seat they would have to clean it up. I told them to let the dog search the other vehicle that is where he wanted. One of the officers told me to shut up they were handling this. I said, "y'all go ahead and do it but I can do a better job." Then one looked at me and said "what is de doing not handcuffed" and I said, "I'm not arrested yet I haven't done anything." He said, "Do you have anything to say now about what part you played in this." I said "Well I'll go ahead and tell you but you haven't read me my rights." They said "put them in the back seat and don't put them together." They put the other guy in a car so we wouldn't talk to each other. I looked at him and made a motion for him to keep quite and he understood. As they were about to drive me to jail I looked around the parking lot and saw someone else I knew was watching the whole scene. The other spectator said it looked as if they were having a police convention. There were at least fifty police cars with all their lights on. On the way to jail I told the policeman that the handcuffs were too tight and could he not hit so many bumps in the road. After getting to jail they put me in a conference room so they could question me. Three policemen came in to question me and they knew me. They said "you know the routine so I'm going to read you your rights." They asked me if I had anything to say. I was already pissed because they blew the customs deal. I said "no" then I said, "Wait a minute I might". They all came back to the table and sat in front of me and leaning over to hear me good. I told them "here is what I have to tell you and listen good." In their excitement they turned on their recorder. I said, "you lack the intelligence, the capacity nor the resources of someone like me to help you." Right after saying that the main interviewer said "I'm going to do everything I can to hurt you." They gave me my one phone call and hung the phone up before the call went through then put me in a holding cell.

There was another person in the holding cell with me and another holding cell must have had about fifteen in it. They didn't have room to sit down. I knew the deputy so I yelled to him to get this guy out of here. I want to be by myself. They took him out of the cell I was in. I told them I still needed a phone call because the first one didn't count and I want to be bonded out of here.

They impounded my truck and held it for thirty days. They also got me in trouble with my job to where I lost my benefits. He also caused my wife to lose her job however I would not give into them and I retained an attorney. After thirty-five days I called the district attorney's office and told them that I wanted my truck released. I owed a lot of storage fees on it and if they wouldn't pay for it I wanted my truck back. They made me pay over $700 cash before they would release my truck. They held my driver's license with my wallet and wouldn't give them back so I had to get a new driver's license. Finally after two months they gave my license back to my attorney. The guy that was caught along with me was continuously begged by the cops to say that I had given him the drugs. They told him that I would kill him and there wasn't anything that I wouldn't do to him. After a few months, the assistant district attorney personally told any law enforcement agency that he could think of to not allow me assist them in any narcotics bust to get out of my charges. He did not like my on a personal and work related basis. I guess he knew that I knew too much about him. After a few big things I ran across in the areas that were a lot larger then me I could see that they had all gotten the word. I knew I was innocent and I had a statement from the boy that was in my favor so I decided to fight it in court.

One Wednesday in August of 2000 I received a phone call from a member of the Harrison County Organized Crime and Drug Enforcement Division. He said that I could help him on a case in Houston that he was told I knew about. I told him I don't know if I can help you or not but someone called me and offered to sell me a large amount of narcotics in Houston. He then told me a boy from Alexandria was arrested and faced thirty-five years in prison. He said if I could help him with the narcotics bust he would try to get his years reduced. I got assurance from him also that if I helped him out he would in turn help me. We left on Thursday morning and we arrived in Houston on Thursday night. I told the police officers the circumstances with my case to and he said he would handle that too. We had to put off the person that we would buy cocaine from until the next day. The agent that would work undercover with said for me to call him the next day at 1:00 p.m. from the Laquinta Hotel. After calling

R he showed up at the hotel to meet the agent and myself. I had never met him myself but he had come to Alexandria before and was selling to a girl in Alexandria. After meeting him at 12:00 p.m. we ordered five kilos of cocaine and 100 lbs. of marijuana. He said that amount would be no problem. We waited in the room from 10 a.m. – 5 p.m. waiting for something to happen. I had conversations with R and his wife about why it was taking so long. He kept saying that he couldn't bring it all at one time so agent E took the next door room so nothing bad would happens as we were giving them another chance to deliver the drugs. R called at 4 p.m. and said he could bring us two kilos at first and if that went well he would bring us more. We waited again and about 4:45 p.m. I called him back and his wife answered. She told me not to leave that R was on his way. By this time the Lieutenant in head of operations said "that's it, let's shut this down". He suspected this would turn out to be a robbery. At 5 p.m. I was telling the agent to get off the phone and leave and a knock came at the door. I looked through the peephole and there was R. I didn't see anyone with him and he said, "hurry and let me in. I can't stand out here with all this stuff." I asked the agent if I should open the door and he nodded his head yes. I started to undo the clasp without actually opening the door and the next thing I knew someone knocked the door in. The force of the door hit me and knocked me on the bed. Two black guys came in with automatic guns shooting at us. The agent had a pistol and positioned himself near the bathroom to avoid being hit. I was lying on the bed and one guy was shot and ran to get next to me and used me for cover to shoot at the guys. All I could hear was bullets then I heard the agent fall. I could hear and feel bullet casings falling on me and I knew I was shot. This was all happening on video. No other officers had shown up for assistance. The agent that was shot was lying on the floor and the drugs dealers assumed he was dead. They grabbed me by the collar of my shirt and put the gun to my head. They asked me where the money was. They knew it should have been in a blue bag so they kept asking me where the blue bag was. I didn't know what to say at first then I told them the blue bag was in a white truck outside. The one that was holding the gun to my head said, "Well let's go get it." I told them I wasn't going out first because we were told earlier by R that if we walked out first we would automatically be shot because R would know something had went wrong. He told his buddy that shot the policeman to go see where the white truck was. I guess you can say it was my luck because there were three white trucks in the parking lot. The guy that went out to look for the truck saw the police coming and ran back into the room telling his buddy that had the gun to my head that the police were coming. They were trying to close the door and lock it and I was thinking the whole time that I couldn't be in this room any longer and be their hostage. I grabbed the door and opened it so the police could come in and while doing this I was shot and fell to the floor between the bed and the air conditioner. The guy that shot me left the door open and starting shooting at he police. He looked back at me one last time to see if I was dead and I held my eyes still and my mouth wide opened holding my breath. He then jumped over the second story balcony and the police were shooting at him on his way down. He had fallen face down on the concrete with the gun still in had with at least eight shots in his body. The other guy threw his gun down and gave up. Then strings of policemen came into the room. One police pointed the gun at my forehead and demanded me not to move or he would shoot. He told me please move and give me any reason to move so I can shoot you. The whole time I was begging them not to shoot me I told them I was on their side and they needed to check the other officer to see if he was all right. They first handcuffed the guy that gave up and kicked the guy in his head with their boots. They then picked me up off the floor and proceeded to handcuff me and I was asking why are you doing this. The officer that was trying to handcuff me had trouble and I was a big guy and another walked over and said, "I'll show you how to loosen him up." He then hit me in my stomach with his fists and then handcuffed me. More officers started punching me after I was handcuffed and shoved me against the window knocking my teeth out. They then dragged me down the stairs and threw me on the pavement. After a few more punches and kicks they threw me in back of a police car. The back of the police car was too small and I was stuck between the front and back seats. They then pulled me out of this car and shoved me into a larger car with a glass divider between the seats. As soon as I was put in this car they turned the engine off so I wouldn't have any air conditioning. I was in this car about three hours handcuffed with no air and in the middle of August. The only thing I could smell was burning flesh, which was my gunshot wound and I was worried I would have a heat stroke. Every now and then an emergency personnel would walk by and give me a drink of water while sharing it with all the other officers. One time they came by the window and I bumped my head against the window asking for more water and he looked at me and gave me the finger. The second time I motioned for water a police officer was carrying it and he pulled his pistol and pointed it at me and told me to shut up. I was in this shape until 8 p.m. that same day when a captain on the homicide squad from the Houston Police Department and asked why were they doing this to me. I couldn't talk or answer him because of heat exhaustion and lack of water. He and another officer helped me out of the car and took the handcuffs off. Emergency personnel took my shirt off to wring it out and when he did he told the detective that I had been shot. He then took off my undershirt and saw the bullet hole then saw where the bullet entered my back and then exited. He asked me who shot me and I told him I didn't know that it could have been a rook or a policeman. They took my shirt for evidence and wiped the blood off my back. He said this is a flesh wound so we aren't going to send you to the hospital. He allowed me to get myself together then he would ask me some question. I stood outside the car as the family came to identify the deal person on the pavement. They all walked by me spitting and cursing me. I believe they thought I had something to do with it. A local T.V. station wanted to talk to me but the cops wouldn't allow them. I wished I could have told them my story.

I had to stand outside so they could take pictures of my back but they wouldn't take any pictures of my other injuries. I could have easily had a worse gunshot wound and died in the back seat of the car and they would not have known. It was after dark before we left the scene. Every vehicle in back of the hotel was shot up. One vehicle wasn't shot and that was mine. One police was looking around and fussing because his truck was shot up and not the one parked next to him was mine. Half of the hotel building was shot up and forty some shots were shot in the room. We were brought from the scene to the Houston City police station for interrogation. There I was questioned and observed the film of what took place. It showed everything but then it seemed the film had been cut or taped over. I asked them where was the part where I was beaten and why was that part cut out. The officer said that he didn't want to blow my cover. I found out later that three men actually came to the room and R took off running and left the other two guys there to kill us and take the money. With forty to eighty policemen supposedly watching the room how can three armed men make it to the second floor without being seen by the officers? I believe the police were very negligent in Houston and Louisiana. I believe Houston didn't watch the room properly nor should they have brutalized me like they did. As far as the police helping me on my case, I doubt they did because the local police had them believing that I had set up the whole deal to rob the Harrison County of over $165,000. This is obnoxious attitude that I received locally. I had to testify against two of the robbers, which I am glad I did. But, I was told do not tell anyone that I was beaten and they would eventually pay me. I don't know where the money went because I only received a very small amount from victim's rights in Texas. I did not receive near the compensation that I should have gotten and I know that there is still the film of the whole incident at the Harrison County police department.

The story ends here, for my wonderful friend died suddenly of a heart attack. Was it from stress and strain or from sheer excitement of the life he led. We will never know but he will be sadly missed.

About the Author

This an autobiography of the events in the life of Gary Lee Bordelon. A life as a Louisiana State Trooper and a Louisiana State Narcotic Agent. On January 4th, 2004, after watching LSU, Louisiana State University, defeat Oklahoma State for the National Football Championship, he pulled out his folder and said, "I need to put this book in order and get it published". Then, he went to bed and was found the next morning on the floor, dead, of a massive heart attack. A death of a good man, husband, and police officer, and the work that he did for the local and state Louisiana police, and the Houston State Police in bring down drug dealers, goes down in this, "Shades of Grey". He will always be in our hearts.